JUMP-START
THE NEXT
GENERATION

JUMP-START
THE NEXT
GENERATION

WILLIAM ROLLINGS

JUMP-START THE NEXT GENERATION

iUniverse books may be ordered through booksellers or by contacting:

iUniverse
1663 Liberty Drive
Bloomington, IN 47403
www.iuniverse.com
1-800-Authors (1-800-288-4677)

ISBN: 978-1-4917-4897-8 (sc)
ISBN: 978-1-4917-4898-5 (e)

Library of Congress Control Number: 2014918199

Printed in the United States of America.

iUniverse rev. date: 10/24/2014

Unless otherwise specified, all Bible verses listed in this work are from the New International Version (NIV).

Contents

Foreword

Imagine a tool that bridges the generational gap/divide by encouraging dialogue around God's Word. The wait has ended with William's devotional *Jump-Start for the Next Generation.* In today's society, the methods by which youth receive "the latest news" are ever-expanding, while the ways they are willing to receive the Word are seemingly dwindling. This collection of devotionals intentionally ensures that youth not only have a rock-solid vehicle in which they can get to God's truths, it also calls adults to the table to facilitate the conversation. With his use of contemporary language, William has made a connection with the next generation.

I'm convinced that it is critical that we all introduce or return our children to the only thing that truly binds one generation to another: scripture. You will find that the format of these devotionals; *Study, Pray, and Share,* are direct, clear, and applicable. This devotional guide fosters and encourages the building of relationships, particularly between the younger generation and those more seasoned among us.

God has used William in a great way during the construction of this book, and I celebrate in advance what it will do for and through you.

Bryan L. Carter
Senior pastor, Concord Church

Preface

How It All Came About

God has blessed me with two beautiful daughters—Alexis and Alyssa. More than anything else, I want to see my daughters trust in Jesus Christ alone as their personal Savior and reach their God-given potential in life. As their father, God has blessed me with the privilege to participate in their spiritual development. Psalm 78:1–4 encourages us to "tell the next generation the praiseworthy deeds of the Lord, his power, and the wonders he has done." Originally, my primary goal was to create personal notes to be shared with our daughters during our family devotional time. Therefore, my effort to reach the next generation was limited to my children. As I started writing the notes, I felt that God was leading me in a new direction. I wondered how this valuable information could benefit other adults and young people. At that point, my efforts evolved from simply writing personal notes for my family into writing the book you know as *Jump-Start the Next Generation*.

Why This Book Is Needed Now

On a daily basis, young people will face the consequences associated with drugs, sexual activity, alcohol, unsafe diets, uncontrolled anger, low self-esteem, bad language, hanging with the wrong crowd, and more. Without advance preparation and adequate support, young people will make decisions that they may regret later in life. *Jump-Start the Next Generation* will equip teens and preteens with the biblical insight they need to make smart choices now and reach their God-given potential in life. Parents and other caring adults will be equipped with an easy-to-use resource to impact the next generation for Christ.

How to Use This Book

Deuteronomy 11:18–21 states, "Fix these words of mine in your hearts and minds; tie them as symbols on your hands and bind them on your foreheads. Teach them to your children, talking about them when you sit at home and when you walk along the road, when you lie down and when you get up. Write them on the doorframes of your houses and on your gates." During this time, people were encouraged to incorporate God's Word into every aspect of their lives. Families would often sit down together and talk about God on a daily basis.

When I wrote *Jump-Start the Next Generation*, I envisioned parents and their children coming together as a team to do three things: study God's Word together, pray together, and share their personal experiences. To facilitate this vision, each devotional lesson is divided into three sections— Study, Pray, and Share. As you begin with the Study section, review the various Bible verses to explore what God has to say about each issue. After you've studied His Word, move to the Pray section. Use the model prayer in this section as a guide to help you pray together. Lastly, end your time together in the Share section. This section allows you to discuss how God has personally helped you navigate through the issue at hand. It can be very rewarding to bring the Bible "closer to home" as you discuss how God has guided you through life's tough situations.

Can you see the vision too? Can you see the adults and young people studying, praying, and sharing together? I pray that God will bless you richly as you take this journey together.

William Rollings

Acknowledgments

I would like to express my sincere thanks to:

My God, Lord and Savior Jesus Christ—for establishing the vision and provision for this book. Your timing is always perfect. I couldn't have completed this book without You. You are the vine; I am the branch; and apart from You, I can do nothing.

My wife, Grenna Rollings—for being an outstanding wife, mother, best friend, and the woman of my dreams. Thank you for all the sacrifices you make for our family. I admire your strong faith and ability to "speak life" over every situation.

My daughters, Alexis and Alyssa Rollings—for making me the proudest father in the world. I am so grateful to have two beautiful daughters like you. You inspired me to write this book, and I dedicate it to you. You will always be Daddy's girls.

My parents, William Sr. and Estic, and my brother, Tedrick Rollings—for your love, encouragement, and unwavering support over the years.

My extended family in Dallas: Bobby, Tannia, and Austin Flewellen—for always encouraging me to follow my dreams.

My family in South Africa—for your long-distance prayers and support. Thanks for allowing me to be a member of the Fynn family.

My pastor, Rev. Bryan Carter—for being a good friend, accountability partner, and outstanding senior pastor. Your humility, lifestyle, and transparency serve as sources of encouragement for others.

My friends and support network, Steve and Kimberly Webb, Charles and Jessica Weaver, Jamaal Wilson, Lee Hampton Jr., and V. Ray Schufford—for your support and words of praise for the book.

Words of Praise for *Jump-Start the Next Generation*

"In *Jump-Start the Next Generation*, author William Rollings has created a powerful "must have" tool needed in the arsenal of every parent with a preteen or teenage child. The book's devotional and discussion format helps break down the walls of communication that have historically hindered parents' ability to openly discuss challenging topics with their children. As a mutually shared devotional between parent and child, *Jump-Start the Next Generation* provides parents with the opportunity to share their own life challenges and testimonies through a series of skillfully crafted daily devotionals, all centered on popular topics and featuring practical biblical nuggets of wisdom."

Steven Webb, MBA
Kimberly Webb, JD, author and speaker

"We really enjoyed this devotional book; it's very driven toward two concepts—spiritual growth and the education of children. We were inspired to finally see a children's book that reaches forward to not only enlighten but also motivate a child to want to know more about how to apply the Word of God in daily life. We love the active engagement that allows our child to share experiences related to subject matters, such as social media, drugs, language, and health. We imagine a dialogue beginning where as a family we hear the concerns of our child; discuss the scripture and study it; and then apply it to the shared experience. The prayer at the end of each devotional sets the tone for our child to seek out more devotional and Bible-driven literature, especially the Bible itself. This book is a definite must-have when spiritually developing our children!"

Charles Weaver, owner, Endurasys Strength Training
Jessica Dixon Weaver, Asst. Professor of Law, Southern Methodist University Dedman School of Law

"*Jump-Start the Next Generation* is going to change the life of every young person who reads this devotional. Brother William Rollings does an excellent job of addressing, in a biblical context, many of the issues that are destroying the moral character and self-worth of teenagers and young adults. By embracing and following the biblical principles explained in *Jump-Start the Next Generation*, our young people are sure to avoid the pitfalls that sidetracked many of us on life's journey."

Jamaal Wilson, Chartered Life Underwriter (CLU),
Wilson Financial Services

"*Jump-Start the Next Generation* is a powerful and practical guide for today's youth. William's insight into modern culture and his application of God's timeless Word to these times is masterful. The book is organized in a brilliant fashion, targeting the very crux of the issues plaguing our youth today. It is real talk in plain English that youth of all ages can absorb. For parents, it provides a perfect launch point for family dinner table discussions."

Lee A. Hampton Jr.
Owner, Victory Custom Homes, Houston, Texas

"William Rollings flat out nailed it when he wrote *Jump-Start the Next Generation*. As a mentor, I know firsthand the importance of relationship and encouragement and the role those two play in aiding youth through these challenging and changing times. *Jump-Start the Next Generation* embodies those attributes and so much more, as a devotional help guide, to equip and add life to a so-called dying generation. This book, I guarantee, will change lives for years to come."

V. Ray Schufford, youth speaker and author

Adversity

Consider it pure joy, my brothers and sisters,
whenever you face trials of many kinds,
because you know that the testing of your faith
produces perseverance. Let perseverance finish its work so that
you may be mature and complete, not lacking anything.

James 1:2–4

Responding to Adversity—Part 1

And we know that in all things God works for the good of those
who love him, who have been called according to his purpose.

Romans 8:28

Study

We can learn about God. All of us will go through a tough time at some
point in our lives. During our tough times, we can learn about God. When
we're sick, we learn that God is a healer. When we're being mistreated by
others, we learn that God is our protector. Whenever we consider our
needs, we learn that God is our provider. While reading Hebrews 13:5,
we are reminded that God stands by our side even during tough times.
Also, Romans 8:28 teaches us that God is in control and He can bring
something positive out of our tough times.

We can increase our faith. James 1:2–3 reminds us that God can use our
tough times to strengthen our faith in Him. Knowing that we can't make
it through the tough times on our own, we quickly learn to depend on
God. As stated in 2 Corinthians 1:8–9:

> We do not want you to be uninformed, brothers and
> sisters, about the troubles we experienced in the province
> of Asia. We were under great pressure, far beyond our
> ability to endure, so that we despaired of life itself. Indeed,
> we felt we had received the sentence of death. But this
> happened that we might not rely on ourselves but on God.

We can learn to persevere. Romans 5:3–5 states, "Suffering produces
perseverance." Many people feel like quitting when life gets tough. God

can use our tough times to teach us how to persevere. Perseverance is our ability to move forward in life although we feel like giving up. If we quit when times get tough, we fail to allow God the opportunity to demonstrate His power in the midst of our struggle. As a result, we may miss God's blessings.

Share

- Describe a time when you persevered through a tough situation.
- What did you learn about God during your tough situation?
- If you are going through a tough time right now, seek encouragement and support from other Christians, and ask God to give you the ability to persevere.

Pray

Lord, whenever I face a tough situation, I pray that You will work everything out for my good. I pray that You will bring something good out of my tough situations. I thank You for being willing to stand by me at all times. Increase my faith, and allow me to learn more about You during my difficult experiences. Give me the strength to persevere, and never quit whenever I face a tough situation. Amen.

Responding to Adversity—Part 2

Consider it pure joy, my brothers and sisters, whenever you face
trials of many kinds, because you know that the testing of your
faith produces perseverance. Let perseverance finish its work so
that you may be mature and complete, not lacking anything.

James 1:2–4

Study

We can grow spiritually. James 1:2–4 teaches us that God can use our
tough times to help us become "mature and complete." It is easy to ignore
God when everything in life is going well. However, our tough times can
drive us closer to God. During our tough times, we are more likely to pray
and study God's Word than ever before. Psalm 119:71 states, "It was good
for me to be afflicted so that I might learn your decrees."

We can rely on God's track record in our lives. As stated in 2 Corinthians
1:10–11, "He has delivered us from such a deadly peril, and He will deliver
us. On Him, we have set our hope that He will continue to deliver us."
The apostle Paul believed that if God helped him through a tough time
before, then He is able to do it again. Once God brings us through one
difficult situation, it gives us the confidence that He's able to do it again
in the future.

We can repent of our sins. Psalm 119:67 states, "Before I was afflicted I
went astray, but now I obey your word." God can use our tough times to
make us aware of any actions that are hindering our walk with Him. Our
tough moments can encourage us to look in the mirror and identify any
changes we need to make in our lives.

We can help others make it through the storms. As 2 Corinthians 1:3–4 reminds us, "We can comfort those in any trouble with the comfort we ourselves receive from God." God can use our struggles to create a personal testimony that we can share with others. We can tell others that if God is able to bring us through the tough times, He is also able to do the same for them too. God comforts us so that we can comfort others.

Share

- Describe how you have grown spiritually during a tough situation.
- Identify a family member or friend this week to encourage during a tough situation
- Read additional Bible verses: 1 Peter 5:10–11 and Romans 5:3.

Pray

Lord, I pray that You will use my tough times to help me grow spiritually. Encourage me to always pray and study Your Word even during the tough times. I know that You are able to see me through any tough situation. Help me to repent of any thoughts or actions that hinder my walk with You. As You bring me through my tough situations, remind me to encourage and support others as they go through their tough situations. Use me to comfort others as You comfort me. Amen.

Anger

A fool gives full vent to his anger,
but a wise man keeps himself under control.

Proverbs 29:11

The Impact of Anger

My dear brothers, take note of this: Everyone should be quick to
listen, slow to speak and slow to become angry, for man's anger
does not bring about the righteous life that God desires.

James 1:19–20

Study

Anger may hurt our reputation. Anger can be defined as a strong feeling
of annoyance, displeasure, or hostility. It is often expressed through yelling,
slamming doors, verbal attacks, physical attacks, and other violent means.
We tend to get angry when things do not turn out as planned and when
we are hurt by the words and actions of others. Because uncontrolled anger
often leads to undesirable behavior, people may avoid being our friend. We
want to avoid being known as a troublemaker. Proverbs 22:24–25 states,
"Do not make friends with a hot-tempered man, do not associate with one
easily angered, or you may learn his ways."

Anger can lead to bigger problems. When we're angry, a simple conflict
can easily lead to something much worse—a serious injury or even the
death of another person. According to the Youth Risk Behavior Surveillance
Report, 16.6 percent of students have carried a weapon; 32.8 percent have
been in a physical fight; 20.1 percent have been bullied; and 5.9 percent of
students didn't go to school because they felt unsafe.[1] Due to anger, many
young people are faced with school suspensions, jail time, and criminal
records.

Anger leads to regret. Proverbs 14:17 reminds us that anger can lead to
foolish acts. After we become angry, we may regret our actions. We may
ask ourselves, "Why did I do that?" At that point, we realize that we could

have handled the situation differently. It is a good idea to think about the consequences of our actions before it is too late. In the heat of the moment, we want to keep our cool. Proverbs 29:11 states, "A fool gives full vent to his anger, but a wise man keeps himself under control."

Share

- Think about a time when you were angry in the past. How could you have handled the situation differently?
- Identify at least one method that you can use the next time you become angry. Here are a few suggestions: remain calm; walk away; pray; reflect on a Bible verse; and hold your breath and count to ten.
- Read additional Bible verses: Proverbs 15:18 and Ecclesiastes 7:9.

Pray

Lord, show me how to handle my emotions in a manner that is pleasing to You. During the heat of the moment, please protect me from saying or doing something that I may regret later. Remind me that uncontrolled anger can be hurtful to others. If I ever become angry, teach me how to resolve my anger as quickly as possible. Let me be quick to apologize if my anger hurts others. Amen.

Beauty

I praise you because I am fearfully and wonderfully
made; your works are wonderful,
I know that full well.

Psalm 139:14

Beauty

But the Lord said to Samuel, "The Lord does not look
at the things people look at. People look at the outward
appearance, but the Lord looks at the heart."

1 Samuel 16:7

Study

The world's perspective on beauty. In "The Real Truth about Beauty Study," only 4 percent of women and 11 percent of girls around the world considered themselves beautiful.[2] Some people believe that beauty is only defined by their physical appearance, such as body weight, skin complexion, hair type, and eye color. As a result, girls and women often have a negative image of their bodies. When it comes to physical attractiveness, the media set unrealistic standards that one can never achieve. Furthermore, we frequently receive the message that being very thin is the best way to go. As a result, many young girls feel insecure about their bodies. Young girls will often seek unhealthy practices to achieve the ideal body, such as anorexia and the use of laxatives.

God's perspective on beauty. Beauty goes beyond physical attractiveness. It's about who you are as a person. Many people will pay close attention to their outer appearances but ignore their inner selves. God wants us to be beautiful on the inside too. If we want to understand beauty from God's perspective, then we should turn to His Word. Proverbs 31:3 states, "Charm is deceptive, and beauty is fleeting; but a woman who fears the Lord is to be praised." Galatians 5:22–23 encourages us to be loving, joyful, peaceful, patient, kind, good, faithful, gentle, and self-controlled. We can also enhance our internal beauty by serving others, praying, and living a godly lifestyle.

Share

- Identify two to three inner qualities that make you a beautiful person on the inside. Here are a few suggestions: kindness, love, gentleness, patience, compassion, generosity, humility, dependability, consideration, and honesty.
- Identify any inner qualities that need to be improved.

Pray

Lord, remind me that I am fearfully and wonderfully made. Help me to understand beauty from Your perspective. Help me to focus on internal beauty by being loving, joyful, peaceful, patient, kind, good, faithful, gentle, and self-controlled. Amen.

Compassion

Be kind and compassionate to one another, forgiving
each other, just as in Christ God forgave you.

Ephesians 4:32

Showing Compassion toward Others

Therefore, as God's chosen people, holy and dearly loved, clothe yourselves with compassion, kindness, humility, gentleness, and patience.

Colossians 3:12

Study

We must look beyond ourselves. Compassion can be defined as caring about people who are facing tough times and having a desire to help them. On a daily basis, we see people who are faced with tough situations: poverty, sickness, hunger, unemployment, financial problems, family problems, and natural disasters. Unfortunately, we live in a selfish world where many people are only concerned about the issues and problems that impact them personally. It is so easy to look at someone who is going through a tough time and say, "Why should I care? It's not my problem." However, God wants us to look beyond ourselves and show concern for others. Also, we must put compassion into action by actually helping others when we can. We may not be able to help everyone, but we can help someone.

Our God is compassionate. We are inspired to be compassionate because we serve a God who is compassionate. Psalm 116:5 states, "The Lord is gracious and righteous; our God is full of compassion." In God's Word, we can find several examples of Jesus's compassion toward others. For example, Jesus showed compassion to people who were helpless (Matthew 9:36), sick (Matthew 14:14), and hungry (Matthew 15:32). Since God shows compassion to others, we should do the same. Ephesians 4:32 states, "Be kind and compassionate to one another."

Share

- Describe a time when you showed compassion to another person.
- Discuss an occasion when someone showed compassion to you. How did it make you feel?

Pray

Lord, thank You for being a compassionate God who cares about others. Because You care about others, touch my heart so that I may care about other people too. Lord, help me to look beyond myself and show compassion to others. Amen.

Decision Making

Show me your ways, Lord, teach me your paths.
Guide me in your truth and teach me,
for you are God my Savior, and my hope is in you all day long.

Psalm 25:4–5

Seek God's Perspective

He guides the humble in what is right and teaches them his way.

Psalm 25:9

Study

Seek advice from other Christians. Proverbs 15:22 states, "Plans fail for lack of counsel, but with many advisers they succeed." When making decisions, we can seek advice from other Christians, especially those who have experience in our area of interest. We can learn from the successes and mistakes of other Christians. Listening to their advice can help us make good decisions and avoid mistakes too. It is hard to make godly decisions when we rely upon ungodly advice. Proverbs 12:5 states, "The plans of the righteous are just, but the advice of the wicked is deceitful."

Seek advice from God through His Word. When making decisions, we can always seek God's Word for advice. Psalm 119:24 states, "Your statutes are my delight; they are my counselors." God's Word will always lead us in the right direction. Psalm 119:105 states, "Your word is a lamp to my feet and a light on my path." As we read God's Word, we can learn from those biblical characters that made good decisions and not-so-good decisions. We can trust God's Word, because it is reliable, credible, and truthful.

Seek advice from God through prayer. As we make decisions, God is always available to give us guidance when we pray. Although God is fully aware of our situation, He still expects us to pray. As we pray, it shows God that we are dependent upon Him. Whenever we're in a hurry, it is easy to skip prayer and make decisions without God's counsel. Unfortunately, hasty decisions can lead to bad results.

Share

- Identify a specific area in your life where you need guidance right now.
- Specify at least two people whom you can trust to give you good advice whenever you need to make a decision.
- Find and become familiar with Bible verses that are related to your specific situation.

Pray

Lord, as I make decisions, I seek Your guidance and direction. On my own, I'm incapable of knowing what's best for me. You are the only one who truly knows what's best for me. I trust that You will always lead me in the right direction. Use Your Word as a lamp to my feet and a light to my path. Surround me with other Christian people who can provide godly advice when needed. Help me to learn from the successes and failures of others. Thank You for allowing me to seek Your guidance when I need to make decisions. Amen.

Understand the Impact—Part 1

The wisdom of the prudent is to give thought to their ways.

Proverbs 14:8

Study

Consider the positive and negative outcomes. Before we make decisions, we should think about the positive and negative outcomes. It is so easy to ignore the negative outcomes and only focus on the positive. For example, hanging out with the in-crowd can be a cool idea but not if those people embrace ungodly behavior. Dating the cutest guy or girl in school may seem exciting but not if that person is a bad influence. We can avoid some painful experiences in life by thinking about the negative outcomes before we make a decision.

Think about the future. We live in a world that encourages us to live for the moment. Before we make a decision, we should ask ourselves, "How will this decision impact me in the future?" We must remember that the outcomes of our decisions may last for months or even years. For example, getting involved with drugs, alcohol, or crime today can make life more difficult for us in the future. Refusing to study hard and be a good student in school could make it difficult to get accepted into college or get a job one day. We must look beyond today and consider how our decisions will impact us in the future.

Share

- Describe a time when you made a decision without first thinking about the outcomes.
- Give an example of a decision that you can make now that will have a positive impact on your future.

Pray

Lord, help me to trust You as I make decisions. You have all wisdom, and You know the outcome of every decision. Give me the courage to take a different course of action when I'm heading in the wrong direction. Help me to make decisions that will lead to the best results. Amen.

Understand the Impact—Part 2

The wisdom of the prudent is to give thought to their ways.

Proverbs 14:8

Study

Understand the impact on others. When making decisions, we should ask ourselves, "Who will be impacted by my decision, and how will it impact them?" We should think very carefully about making any decisions that will have a negative impact on others. For example, if we decide to drive a car while drinking alcohol or sending a text message, that decision can harm others. If we decide to be mean or tease others, that decision will create an unpleasant experience for the other person. We want to make decisions that will make life better for others—not worse.

Understand the spiritual impact. Knowing that God is with us at all times, we should make decisions that will please Him. We should ask ourselves, "How will this decision bring glory to God's name?" Colossians 3:17 states, "And whatever you do, whether in word or deed, do it all in the name of the Lord Jesus." If we want God's input before making a decision, we can pray about the situation and read His Word. We can also seek advice from other Christians and our parents.

Share

- Describe a time when you made a decision that hurt someone else.
- Describe a time when you made a decision that had a positive impact on someone else.
- Ask God to help you make good decisions each day.

Pray

Lord, I know that You are with me at all times. Help me to make decisions that will please You. Help me to think about others as I make decisions. Lead me to make decisions that will bring glory and honor to Your name. Amen.

Drugs and Alcohol

Do not join those who drink too much wine.

Proverbs 23:20

Alcohol Is a Problem

Do not get drunk on wine, which leads to
debauchery. Instead, be filled with the Spirit.

Ephesians 5:18

Study

Alcohol can become a problem for many young people. At least 70.8
percent of students have had at least one drink of alcohol in their lifetime,
and 21.9 percent of students have participated in binge-drinking, where
they've consumed five or more alcoholic drinks in one setting.[3]

Know the influences. Young people may get involved with alcohol for
various reasons, including a desire to fit in with others, have fun, and try
something new. Sweet and fruity alcoholic drinks are often used to appeal
to the tastes of younger audiences. Alcohol can be easily accessed at home,
school, parties, and other places where young people hang out. Alcohol
is a favorite drink at many parties and happy-hour events. Young people
are encouraged to believe that alcohol is cool; everybody drinks; and they
should too.

Know the consequences. Proverbs 20:1 states, "Wine is a mocker and beer
a brawler; whoever is led astray by them is not wise." Alcohol may make
people feel good in the moment, but there are consequences to consider.
Under the influence of alcohol, people don't always think as clearly as they
should. Isaiah 28:7 reminds us that alcohol can impact a person's decision-
making abilities. Research indicates that 28 percent of young people killed
in auto crashes are impacted by alcohol.[4] Adolescent drinkers are more
likely to get involved with fights, have unplanned sex, become victims of
sexual assault, and perform worse in school.[5]

We must protect ourselves. We don't want to be in a position where we lose control of ourselves and become mastered by alcohol. In 1 Corinthians 6:12, we are reminded not to be "mastered by anything." Considering the negative consequences, young people should stay away from alcohol. Overall, young people should avoid any situations that might expose them to the harmful effects of alcohol. Proverbs 23:20 states, "Do not join those who drink too much wine."

Share

- If someone encourages you to drink alcohol, how will you respond?
- Make a commitment to remove yourself from the situation if your friends are drinking alcohol.
- If you are in a car with a driver who has been drinking alcohol, call your parents or someone else to give you a ride to your destination.

Pray

Lord, help me to resist any advertisements, friends, or family members that may encourage me to get drunk on alcohol. Keep alcohol out of my home and path. Whenever someone encourages me to drink alcohol, remind me of the negative consequences. Give me the wisdom to hang out with friends who don't get drunk on alcohol. Help me to avoid any parties or events where alcohol may be present. Remind me not to be "mastered by anything." Amen.

Drugs Are a Problem

Do you not know that your bodies are temples of the Holy Spirit, who is in you, whom you have received from God? You are not your own; you were bought at a price. Therefore honor God with your bodies.

1 Corinthians 6:19–20

Study

Be aware of illegal drugs. Young people will use drugs for many reasons including peer pressure, rebellion, thrill-seeking, curiosity, and to escape the pressures of life.[6] Common drugs used by adolescents include marijuana, club drugs, LSD (acid), cocaine, methamphetamines (meth), and heroin. Club drugs, such as ecstasy, are used at concerts, nightclubs, and parties. Marijuana has been a widely used illicit drug; at least 30 percent of twelfth graders reported using it at least once[7] and over 80 percent stating that it is very easy to gain access to the drug.[8]

Watch out for "harmless" drugs. Many young people are moving beyond the illegal drugs to abuse prescription drugs, like painkillers. These drugs are "legal" and can be found in the medicine cabinet at home. Also, young people are using inhalants to inhale chemical vapors to get high.[9] Inhalants can be found in common household products, such as nail polish remover, correction fluid, and spray paint.

Know the consequences. In 1 Corinthians 6:19–20, we are reminded that our bodies belong to God. Therefore, we want to avoid any activity that causes harm to our bodies. Similar to alcohol, drugs may make us feel good in the moment, but there are consequences. Many drug users have experienced heart failure, strokes, seizures, amnesia, unconsciousness, violent behavior, anxiety, and increased blood pressure.

Say no to drugs. Similar to alcohol, we don't want to be in a position where we lose control of ourselves and become mastered by drugs. In 1 Corinthians 6:12, we are reminded not to be "mastered by anything." Considering the negative consequences, we want our young people to say no to drugs and avoid any people or situations that may expose them to drugs.

Share

- If someone encourages you to use drugs, how will you respond?
- Make a commitment to remove yourself from the situation if your friends are using drugs.
- Parents: Move any prescription drugs or other harmful substances out of your children's reach.

Pray

Lord, help me to resist any friends or family members who may encourage me to use drugs. Keep drugs out of my home. Whenever someone encourages me to use drugs, remind me of the negative consequences. Give me the wisdom to spend time with friends who don't use drugs. Guide me to avoid parties or events where I suspect that drugs will be present. Expose me to the truth in Your Word. Remind me not to be "mastered by anything." Amen.

Faith

But blessed is the one who trusts in the Lord,
whose confidence is in him.

Jeremiah 17:7

Keeping the Faith

Now faith is being sure of what we hope for
and certain of what we do not see.

Hebrews 11:1

Study

Be confident in God's ability. Faith can be defined as our trust and confidence in a person or thing. In Matthew 9:27–30, two blind men approached Jesus to have their eyesight restored. In response, Jesus said, "Do you believe that I am able to do this?" Jesus wanted to know if the blind men had faith in His ability to restore their eyesight. Jeremiah 17:7 states, "But blessed is the one who trusts in the Lord, whose confidence is in him." Whenever we make a request to God, we should be confident that He is able to meet our needs.

Keep the faith when life gets tough. James 1:2–4 reminds us that our faith is being tested whenever we go through tough times. As long as everything in life is going as planned, it is much easier to have confidence in God. However, our confidence in God may fade whenever life doesn't turn out as planned. For example, tough times can lead us to doubt God and question if He is able to meet our needs. However, we know that God cares about our lives, and He promises to be with us every step of the way.

The timing isn't what we expected. We live in a world where we expect all our plans and dreams to happen right now. As long as everything is taking place according to our schedule, our confidence in God is strong. However, we shouldn't lose our confidence in God when everything isn't happening as quickly as we'd like. We must remember that God knows what's best for us, and He knows when it is best for us to have it. It is possible that God will allow us to realize our dreams but at a different time.

Share

- Talk about a time when you had to trust God for something.

Pray

Lord, help me to trust You at all times. I pray that I will not place my trust in people or things over You. I place my trust in You alone. Amen.

Fashion

I also want the women to dress modestly, with decency and propriety, adorning themselves, not with elaborate hairstyles or gold or pearls or expensive clothes, but with good deeds, appropriate for women who profess to worship God.

1 Timothy 2:9–10

Fashion

I also want the women to dress modestly, with decency and propriety, adorning themselves, not with elaborate hairstyles or gold or pearls or expensive clothes, but with good deeds, appropriate for women who profess to worship God.

1 Timothy 2:9–10

Study

Be careful about the message we're sending. In 1 Timothy 2:9–10, the Bible isn't stating that a female shouldn't dress fashionably. Instead, the verse encourages people to embrace the concept of modesty. Whether we like it or not, people often make judgments about others based on a person's clothing. A young girl's choice of clothing may send the wrong message, misrepresent her intentions, and attract the wrong type of attention. In an effort to look "grown-up," some young girls may wear short skirts, tight-fitting clothing, short shorts, low-cut tops, and other revealing clothing. As a result, young boys may perceive these girls as very "easy" and readily available for sex.

Young boys should make good choices about their clothing as well. For example, wearing sagging pants and revealing one's underwear can send the wrong message to others. We want both our young girls and boys to carry themselves in a respectable manner.

When in doubt, seek advice. When in doubt, we can always seek feedback about our choice of clothing from godly family members and friends. What a person wears on the outside may not be a true reflection of who he or she is on the inside. However, we must remember that people will first see what's on the outside before they get to know who we are on the inside.

Share

- Identify one to two people whom you can trust to provide good advice about your clothing.
- Go through your closet this week and seek advice concerning the appropriateness of any outfits that may be questionable.

Pray

Lord, help me to give You the glory in everything that I do. Teach me how to dress in a manner that is pleasing to You. I pray that my choice of clothing will send a positive message to others. Amen.

Friends

A friend loves at all times,
and a brother is born for a time of adversity.

Proverbs 17:17

Friends—Part 1

Two are better than one, because they have a good return for
their work: If one falls down, his friend can help him up. But
pity the man who falls and has no one to help him up!

Ecclesiastes 4:9–10

Study

Friends are there when needed. Proverbs 17:17 states, "A friend loves at
all times, and a brother is born for a time of adversity." Friends should be
there for one another during the good times and the tough times. Friends
shouldn't desert one another when life becomes difficult. Whenever we
are faced with tough times, we need friends who will stand by our side.
Among friends, we can openly talk about our fears, challenges, weaknesses,
and disappointments.

Friends help one another grow in our faith. Proverbs 27:17 states, "As
iron sharpens iron, so one person sharpens another." Friends can sharpen
one another by praying together, studying God's Word together, and
holding one another accountable. By surrounding ourselves with the right
friends, we can help one another become better Christians and reach our
God-given potential.

Friendships require effort. Proverbs 18:24 states, "A man who has friends
must himself be friendly." It takes work to maintain good friendships. No
one likes being involved in one-sided friendships where one person puts
forth most of the effort. If we want to have good friendships then we must
be good friends ourselves.

Share

- Do you have any friends who are going through a tough time right now? If so, contact them this week to encourage them.
- Identify at least one friend whom you can pray with on a regular basis.

Pray

Lord, surround me with godly friends so that we can become better Christians. I pray that my friends and I will be there for one another during the good times and the tough times. Encourage me to be a good friend at all times. Amen.

Friends—Part 2

The righteous choose their friends carefully, but
the way of the wicked leads them astray.

Proverbs 12:26

Stay away from the wrong crowd. Proverbs 12:26 reminds us to select our
friends carefully. In some cases, a child's friend can be just as influential as
the child's parents or family members. Therefore, selecting our friends is a
very important decision. Our friends can have either a positive or negative
influence on us. We should avoid friends who will lead us down the wrong
path. According to 1 Corinthians 15:33, "Do not be misled: 'Bad company
corrupts good character.'" It will be difficult to please God when we are
constantly being pulled in the wrong direction by our friends.

Focus on quality, not quantity. It is easy to assume that more is better
when it comes to our friends. However, it is better to have a few friends
who will be a good influence than to have many friends who will be a
negative influence. We shouldn't be disappointed if we aren't the most
popular person in the crowd. We should never compromise our Christian
lifestyle so that we can be accepted by others.

Make contact with non-Christians. It is so easy for many Christians to
spend most of their time with other Christians. However, God also calls
us to share our faith with people who are non-Christians. In the book
Becoming A Contagious Christian, authors Bill Hybels and Mark Mittelberg
state, "So if we're going to impact our world for Christ, the most effective
approach will be through friendships with those who need to be reached."
As we interact with non-Christians, we should demonstrate God's love
toward them and pray that He will touch their hearts one day.

Share

- Do you have any friends who are a bad influence on you? If so, what should you do about your relationship with them?
- Identify at least one non-Christian whom you can get to know better. Strive to be a positive influence on that person.
- Parents: Get to know your child's friends. Encourage your child to gravitate toward those friends who are a positive influence and stay away from those who are a negative influence.

Pray

Lord, give me the wisdom to choose my friends carefully. Help me to stay away from people who will lead me in the wrong direction. I pray that I will never compromise my Christian lifestyle to be accepted by others. Use me to be a godly influence on people who are non-Christians. Amen.

Generosity

A generous person will prosper; whoever
refreshes others will be refreshed.

Proverbs 11:25

Be Generous Toward Others

What good is it, my brothers and sisters, if someone claims to have faith but has no deeds? Can such faith save them? Suppose a brother or a sister is without clothes and daily food. If one of you says to them, "Go in peace; keep warm and well fed," but does nothing about their physical needs, what good is it? In the same way, faith by itself, if it is not accompanied by action, is dead.

James 2:14–17

Study

Take action. The world is filled with people who lack access to the basic things in life—nutritious food, clean drinking water, clothes, and housing. Unfortunately, it is very easy to ignore people who need our help. James 2:14–17 reminds us to take action whenever we see people who are in need. We can help people by sharing our money, belongings, and time. For example, we can donate clothes to the needy or volunteer at food banks and homeless shelters.

Ensure that God receives the glory. Whenever we help others, it should be done for the right reasons. In Matthew 6:1–2, some of the religious people gave to the poor to make themselves look good in front of others. We shouldn't help others in an effort to draw attention to ourselves. As we help others, we want them to ultimately acknowledge God as the one who provides for them. Matthew 5:16 states, "Let your light shine before others, that they may see your good deeds and glorify your Father in heaven."

Don't become discouraged by our limited resources. In 2 Corinthians 8:1–4, we learn about the people of the Macedonian church. Although they were poor, they were eager to support others who needed help. Likewise, we shouldn't become discouraged if we don't have a large amount of money to help others. Instead, we should help others to the best of our ability. As is stated in 2 Corinthians 8:12, "For if the willingness is there, the gift is acceptable according to what one has, not according to what one does not have."

Share

- Find a way to help someone who is in need this month—donate clothes, volunteer at a shelter, help out at a food bank, etc.
- Read additional Bible verses: Deuteronomy 15:7–11; Proverbs 22:9; Psalms 37:26, 112:5; 2 Corinthians 9:10–12; Romans 12:13; and Hebrews 13:16.

Pray

Lord, I know that You are a generous God. Help me to be generous toward others. Remove any selfishness from my heart. I pray that I will help others for the right reasons. When I help people, I pray that they will glorify You. Amen.

Good Health

Dear friend, I pray that you may enjoy good health and that all may go well with you, even as your soul is getting along well.

3 John 1:2

Take Care of Our Bodies

Do you not know that your bodies are temples of the Holy Spirit, who
is in you, whom you have received from God? You are not your own;
you were bought at a price. Therefore honor God with your bodies.

1 Corinthians 6:19–20

Study

Unhealthy eating hurts us. Unhealthy eating can have a negative impact
on our bodies. For example, the consumption of sugary drinks by young
people can lead to obesity if consumed in large amounts.[10] Advertising
plays a key role, since unhealthy foods are often marketed to children.
Also, we must monitor the amount of food we eat. Many kids and adults
will face health risks if they overeat and fail to monitor their portion
sizes.[11] The lack of access to high-quality food can serve as a problem as
well. Many families lack access to grocery stores that sell healthy foods in
their communities.[12]

Lack of physical activity hurts us. Research indicates that young people
should be physically active for at least sixty minutes per day.[13] It is difficult
to stay active when children spend hours sitting at their desks in school
and adults spend hours sitting in front of computers at work. On a daily
basis, children spend at least 4.5 hours watching TV, 1 hour playing video
games, and 1.5 hours on the computer.[14]

We can still make a difference. Despite the statistics, we can take practical
steps to improve our health. For example, we can drink more water instead
of sugary drinks; eat fruit and vegetables as snacks; minimize junk food; and
watch our portion sizes. The American Academy of Pediatrics recommends

that TV usage should be limited to two hours per day.[15] As an alternative to TV and video games, we can increase our daily physical activity.

Share

- How would you describe your eating habits? Start eating right this month.
- How much physical activity and exercise do you get on a regular basis? Make a commitment this week to stay physically active and exercise on a regular basis.
- Read an additional Bible verse: 3 John 1:2.

Pray

Lord, help me to take good care of my body. I pray that I will stay away from foods that are not good for my body. Give me the desire to exercise and stay active every day. Amen.

Humility

Live in harmony with one another. Do not be proud, but be willing to associate with people of low position. Do not be conceited.

Romans 12:16

Be Humble

All of you, clothe yourselves with humility toward one
another, because God opposes the proud but gives grace
to the humble. Humble yourselves, therefore, under God's
mighty hand, that He may lift you up in due time.

1 Peter 5:5–6

Study

When we're humble, we don't think that we are better than other people.
We believe that all people are valuable to God regardless of their race,
gender, wealth, or power. Romans 12:16 states, "Live in harmony with one
another. Do not be proud, but be willing to associate with people of low
position. Do not be conceited." Therefore, we are reminded to have the
right attitude toward other people.

Be humble about our material possessions. We shouldn't think that we
are better than other people because of our money and material possessions.
Deuteronomy 8:18 informs us that God is the one who enables us to have
access to money. Therefore, we should be thankful and have the right
attitude about money and people.

Be humble about our abilities. Whenever we are good at something, we
should see our success as a blessing from God and have the right attitude
about it. We should never think that we are superior to other people
because of our success and ability to do well in certain areas. According
to 2 Corinthians 3:5 it is "not that we are competent in ourselves to claim
anything for ourselves, but our competence comes from God."

Be humble about our spiritual progress. We should never think that we are superior to others because of our spiritual growth. In Luke 18:9–14, the religious man believed that he was superior and more righteous than the other man. We should remember that our spiritual progress is only possible by God's grace.

Share

- Have you ever felt that you were better than someone else? If so, what made you feel that way?
- Have you ever been arrogant about a specific thing that you do well? If so, please share.
- Read additional Bible verses: Proverbs 16:18; Romans 12:16; Psalm 25:9; Luke 18:9–14; Ephesians 2:8–9; Philippians 2:3; and 1 Corinthians 1:26–27.

Pray

Lord, help me to be a person of humility. Remind me to never think that I am superior to other people. I have no reason to brag about myself. You are the source and provider of everything that I have. Give me a humble heart. Amen.

Integrity

Whoever walks in integrity walks securely,
but whoever takes crooked paths
will be found out.

Proverbs 10:9

Do the Right Thing

I know, my God, that you test the heart
and are pleased with integrity.

1 Chronicles 29:17

Study

We can't hide our actions from God. Integrity can be simply defined as doing the right thing. God wants us to do the right thing even if other people aren't aware of our actions. We shouldn't think that it is okay to do the wrong thing as long as no one else knows about it. We can hide our actions from others, but we can't hide from God. God sees and knows everything. Hebrews 4:13 states, "Nothing in all creation is hidden from God's sight. Everything is uncovered and laid bare before the eyes of him to whom we must give account." Proverbs 10:9 reminds us that people who do the right thing have nothing to hide from others.

God is concerned about how we get things done. Some people assume that it doesn't matter how we reach our goals in life as long as we reach them. For example, a person may cheat in school to earn good grades or deceive others to get what he or she wants. However, God is concerned about what we accomplish in life and how we accomplish it. He wants us to reach our goals in a manner that is pleasing to Him.

Integrity goes beyond how we feel about the situation. Many people believe that it is up to each person to determine what's right and what's wrong. For this reason, a person can do the wrong thing but never feel bad about it. However, God is the one who sets the standard about what's right and what's wrong. First Corinthians 4:4 states, "My conscience is clear, but that does not make me innocent. It is the Lord who judges me." If we want to know if an action is right or wrong, we can always seek God's guidance about the matter.

Share

- Give an example of a time when you demonstrated integrity.
- Have you ever done something that you didn't want other people to know about? If so, how did you feel about it?
- Read additional Bible verses: Proverbs 10:9; and Psalms 41:12, 25:21.

Pray

Lord, help me to live a life of integrity at all times. Lord, I know that You are the one who determines what's right and what's wrong. Whenever I want to do the wrong thing, remind me that You are aware of my actions. Help me to please You in everything that I do. Amen.

Language

Do not let any unwholesome talk come out of your mouths,
but only what is helpful for building others up according
to their needs, that it may benefit those who listen.

Ephesians 4:29

Language

May these words of my mouth and this meditation
of my heart be pleasing in your sight.

Psalm 19:14

Study

Avoid profanity and "bad language." Colossians 3:8 reminds us to
avoid "filthy" language. Unfortunately, profanity can be heard in the latest
song, television show, or movie. However, God wants His children to stay
away from such language. James 3:9 states, "With the tongue we praise
our Lord and Father, and with it we curse human beings, who have been
made in God's likeness. Out of the same mouth come praise and cursing.
My brothers and sisters, this should not be."

Avoid negative words that hurt others. Psalm 64:3 states, "They sharpen
their tongues like swords and aim cruel words like deadly arrows."
Unfortunately, our words can hurt others. People often speak cruel
words about another person's physical appearance, race, gender, or family
background. It can be very painful when someone calls you too fat, too
ugly, too skinny, too dumb, etc. God doesn't want us to use words to hurt
others.

Use words that build people up. Instead of using words that tear people
down, Ephesians 4:29 reminds us to use words that build them up. Before
we speak, we can ask ourselves, "How will my words impact the other
person? Will my words make her life better or worse?" We can use our
words to cheer people up, encourage them, celebrate with them when they
succeed, acknowledge their positive attributes, etc.

Speak positive words about ourselves. It will be difficult to experience positive things in our lives when we speak negatively about ourselves. For example, we should avoid making such statements as, "I can't do anything right;" "I will never do well in school;" "I'm ugly;" or "I'm stupid." We should use words that will build ourselves up and not tear ourselves down. Therefore, we must view ourselves from God's perspective and speak words that confirm His thoughts about us.

Share

- Do you believe that it is okay to use profanity? If not, what will you do to avoid using this type of language? Read James 3:9.
- Have you ever used words that hurt someone else? If so, make a commitment to use your words to build people up instead. Read Ephesians 4:29.
- If any, what negative words have you spoken about yourself? Write down two to three positive qualities about yourself, and place them in a visible location in your house for you to see every day.
- Read additional Bible verses: Proverbs 18:21, 12:18; Psalms 19:14, 141:3, 139:4; and Luke 6:45.

Pray

Lord, help me to stay away from negative language that will hurt others. Fill my mouth with positive words that will build others up. Show me how to speak positive words over my own life. Help me to avoid speaking negative words about myself. I pray that I will my words to steer my life in the right direction. Amen.

Media Choices

See to it that no one takes you captive through hollow and deceptive philosophy, which depends on human tradition and the basic principles of this world rather than on Christ.

Colossians 2:8

Choose Our Media Wisely

And whatever you do, whether in word or deed,
do it all in the name of the Lord Jesus.

Colossians 3:17

Study

Monitor our Internet and cell phone usage. Although technology can be used to stay in touch with family and friends, it should be used wisely. For example, we shouldn't use our cell phones while driving, because it is dangerous. We should avoid using the Internet to share inappropriate photos of ourselves, make threats to harm people, or form unhealthy relationships with the opposite sex. We must remember that many schools and businesses will monitor a person's Internet activity when it is time to evaluate prospective students and employees. Therefore, misusing the Internet could hurt our efforts to get into college and get a job. Plus, law enforcement agencies often use the Internet to identify people who are involved in inappropriate activities. Therefore, we must learn to use technology wisely.

Monitor our choice of TV shows and movies. While watching our favorite TV shows and movies, we will be exposed to many messages. The use of sex, drugs, alcohol, violence, and bad language are common in many television shows and movies. First Thessalonians 5:21 reminds us to evaluate every message to ensure that it is aligned with the Word of God. Exposure to the wrong messages can have a negative impact on how we think and act. Therefore, we want to make good choices with our TV shows and movies.

Monitor our choice of music. We also want to make good choices when it comes to our music. Many people will say, "It is only a song. I'm not hurting anybody by listening to it." However, it can be harmful if we expose ourselves to the wrong messages. Also, females are often portrayed in a negative manner in music videos and performances. We have the power to choose our media outlets. We want to stay away from music that degrades people. We want to select media choices that honor God and respect people.

Share

- Do you think that it is okay to send text messages while driving? Make a commitment to never text and drive. It is not worth risking your life or health. You can always send or read the message at another time.
- Do you ever enjoy music, movies, TV shows, or websites that aren't good for you? If so, what do you plan to do about it?
- Parents: Consider buying special software to protect your children against inappropriate Internet content. Review good websites to learn about the appropriateness of movie content before you watch a movie: www.pluggedin.com and www.parentpreviews.com.

Pray

Lord, help me to stay away from any media outlets that will have a negative impact on how I think and act. Give me the wisdom to filter every media message through Your Word. I want to avoid any medium that is disrespectful toward people. I pray that I will only select media outlets that glorify You. Amen.

Money

The wise store up choice food and olive oil,
but fools gulp theirs down.

Proverbs 21:20

Saving Money

The wise store up choice food and olive oil,
but fools gulp theirs down.

Proverbs 21:20

Study

Spend wisely. Although money is required to buy the things that we need and want in life, we must use it wisely. As we receive money, we should first think about how we plan to use it. For example, we can allocate our money into key categories, such as spend, save, and give. When it comes to spending money, it is a good idea to set aside money in advance to buy items later. Before we spend money, we can ask ourselves a few questions: "Do I have enough to buy this item now, or should I wait until later? If I buy this item now, will I have enough money to buy other items that I may need?" It is okay to spend money, but we should do so wisely.

Start saving money early. Spending all our money can cause problems for us. We must save some money too. Saving allows us to set aside money today that we can use at a later time. For example, we may need to save money to pay for sports equipment, musical instruments, school trips, computers, summer camps, college tuition, or an unexpected emergency. It is never too early to start saving money, nor too late. Many parents open savings accounts to encourage their children to start saving money at an early age. Some parents even take their children to the bank to actually deposit the money themselves. We can even learn more about money in fun ways through board games and websites. We should start saving money as soon as possible!

Share

- If you were given $50.00, how would you allocate the money into the three categories: give, save, and spend?
- Parents: Visit a local bank to open a savings account for your child this week.
- Parents: Take three envelopes and label them "give," "spend," and "save." As your child receives money, help him or her allocate those funds into the three categories.

Pray

Lord, help me to start saving money as soon as possible. Encourage me to look beyond today and think about tomorrow as well. Lord, teach me how to be wise in how I spend money. Thank You for being my true Provider. Amen.

Giving Back to God

Honor the Lord with your wealth,
with the first fruits of all your crops.

Proverbs 3:9

Study

God owns all our resources. Psalm 24:1 states, "The earth is the Lord's and everything in it, the world, and all who live in it." God calls us to be good stewards of His resources. Since God is the one who owns the resources, He allows us to take care of them on His behalf. Therefore, we shouldn't say to ourselves, "I earned this money, and no one can tell me how to use it." Since God owns everything, we should give back to Him a portion of what He's given to us. For example, whenever we give our tithes to the local church, we are supporting God's work here on earth.

Give according to your ability. As 2 Corinthians 8:12 states, "For if the willingness is there, the gift is acceptable according to what he has, not according to what he does not have." We shouldn't see our giving to God as a competition with other people. We shouldn't feel guilty if we can't give to God as much as someone else does. We give to please God, not people. God is fully aware of our financial situation. He knows what we can and cannot give. It's our task to do our best with what God has given to us.

Give with the right attitude. According to 2 Corinthians 9:7, "Each man should give what he has decided in his heart to give, not reluctantly or under compulsion, for God loves a cheerful giver." Whenever we give to God, we should do so with the right attitude. The act of giving to God is a reflection of what's in our hearts. God wants us to give because we have a desire to do so. He wants us to give out of our love and appreciation for Him.

Share

- Do you believe that we should give back to God a portion of what He has given to us? Or should we keep it all to ourselves?
- On a regular basis, use the money from your "give" envelope to make an offering at church.
- Parents: In this lesson, the primary focus is on giving back to God. In addition, you may want to encourage your child to give money to support a local charity or good cause.
- Read additional Bible verses: Malachi 3:8–10 and 1 Chronicles 29:14.

Pray

Lord, I believe that You are the source who provides me with everything that I have. Help me to be a good steward of the resources You have provided for me. I pray that I will faithfully give back to You a portion of what You have given to me. Bless me to be a cheerful giver who gives with the right heart. Amen.

Obedience

Teach me, Lord, the way of your decrees, that I may
follow it to the end. Give me understanding, so that I
may keep your law and obey it with all my heart.

Psalm 119:33–34

Obedience—Part 1

Jesus replied, "Anyone who loves me will obey my teaching."

John 14:23

Study

Obeying God demonstrates our love for Him. Obedience can be simply defined as doing what we're told to do. As Christians, God expects us to obey Him. Whenever we obey God, we are sending Him a message that we love Him. John 14:15 states, "If you love me, keep my commands." God has done so much for us, and we want to please Him at all times. Our love for God gives us a reason to obey Him.

Obeying God is good for us. Isaiah 48:17 informs us that God knows what is best for us. Therefore, it is a good idea to obey Him and follow His commands. Obeying God can lead to peace, satisfaction, and other rewards.

Disobeying God should lead us to repent. All of us will make mistakes in life, and God is willing to forgive us. As stated in 1 John 1:9, "If we confess our sins, he is faithful and just and will forgive us our sins." Whenever we disobey God, we should confess our sins and seek His forgiveness. Although confessing our sins is a great first step, God also wants us to take it a step further and actually change our ways. He ultimately wants us to obey Him.

Don't be selective about obeying God. First Thessalonians 5:22 states, "Avoid every kind of evil." Sometimes, we will obey God in one area of our lives but disobey Him in other areas. However, God wants us to obey all His commands—not just the few commands that we like. We shouldn't use our obedience in one area as an excuse to ignore or disobey God in other areas. We should aim to please God in every area of our lives.

Share

- Do you find it more difficult to obey God in certain areas of your life? If so, ask God to help you obey Him in those areas.
- Think about a time when you obeyed God. How did you feel afterward?
- Read additional Bible verses: Psalm 78:1–32 and Proverbs 28:13.

Pray

Lord, because I love You, I want to please You in everything that I do. I can never go wrong by obeying You. Whenever I disobey You, I pray that I will confess my sins to You; seek your forgiveness; and change my actions. Since You know what's best for me, I want to obey You at all times. Amen.

Obedience—Part 2

Children, obey your parents in the Lord, for this is right.
"Honor your father and mother"—which is the first
commandment with a promise—"that it may go well with
you and that you may enjoy long life on the earth."

Ephesians 6:1–4

Study

Obey our parents. God gives parents authority over their children, and He expects the children to obey their parents. Parents are given the responsibility to equip their children to live in a manner that pleases God. As a child, it appears that our parents develop rules and boundaries to stop us from having fun. However, God places parents in the lives of children to protect them, not hurt them. By listening to our parents, we can avoid some of the pitfalls of life. Even if we don't like the rules, God still expects us to obey our parents. Whenever we obey our parents, God is pleased with our actions. Colossians 3:20 states, "Children, obey your parents in everything, for this pleases the Lord."

Honor our parents. Even as we obey our parents, we must do so with the right attitude. In addition to obeying our parents, God also expects us to respect our parents. Ephesians 6:1–2 reminds us to "honor" our parents. The word "honor" means to respect. Some people may believe that it is okay to behave disrespectfully toward their parents. However, God expects us to both obey and respect our parents.

Obey others who have authority. In addition to parents, children are also expected to obey other adults who have authority over them: teachers, principals, coaches, police officers, and pastors. We live in a world where people are constantly behaving disrespectfully toward one another. However, parents should encourage their children to behave respectfully toward all adults who have authority over them.

Share

- Give an example of how you have benefited from obeying your parents.
- Do you find it difficult to obey other adults besides your parents? If so, who and why?
- Put forth the effort this week to obey the adults in your life.

Pray

Lord, help me to obey my parents at all times. I know that You are pleased whenever I obey my parents. As I obey my parents, help me to do so with the right attitude. Show me how to honor and respect my parents as well. Help me to also obey other adults who may have authority as well. Amen.

Passion for
God's Word

My soul is consumed with longing for your laws at all times.

Psalm 119:20

The Benefits of God's Word

Open my eyes that I may see wonderful things in your law.

Psalm 119:18

Study

It helps us know the truth. We live in a world that is filled with untruthful information. However, we can rely upon God's Word to help us know the truth. God is the author of truth, and He never lies to us. Numbers 23:19 states, "God is not human, that he should lie." Psalm 18:30 states, "As for God, his way is perfect; the word of the Lord is flawless."

It provides guidance. Psalm 119:105 states, "Your word is a lamp for my feet, a light on my path." We can use God's Word as a light to help us see things more clearly. God's Word can also help us stay on track and walk down the right path in life. The Bible offers guidance on how we should live.

It protects us against sin. Psalm 119:11 states, "I have hidden your word in my heart that I might not sin against you." Whenever we are tempted to do the wrong thing, we can use God's Word to lead us in the right direction. In Matthew 4:1–11, Jesus Christ was tempted by the enemy to do the wrong thing. However, Jesus used God's Word to help Him do the right thing and defeat the enemy. Likewise, we can use God's Word to fight against sin and do the right thing.

It helps us grow spiritually. Once we become Christians, God wants us to keep growing spiritually. As newborn babies, we needed milk to help us grow physically. Likewise, if we want to grow spiritually, we need a regular intake of God's Word, which serves as our "spiritual milk." We need to be nourished by God's Word on a daily basis so that we can grow.

Share

- Do you need guidance in any area of your life right now? If so, identify Bible verses that address your specific issue.
- Describe a time when you used God's Word to help you do the right thing.
- Read additional Bible verses: 1 Peter 2:1–2 and Psalm 19:7–9.

Pray

Lord, I believe that Your Word is true and right. Help me to use Your Word to fight against sin and stay away from anything that doesn't please You. I pray that I will grow spiritually as I read Your Word on a regular basis. Whenever I need to make a decision, I pray that I will use Your Word to lead me in the right direction. Amen.

Going Deeper in God's Word

My soul is consumed with longing for your laws at all times.

Psalm 119:20

Study

Study and memorize the Bible. Studying God's Word is a good habit. As we study the Bible, we want to ask ourselves, "What does this Bible verse mean, and how do I apply it to my life?" No matter how much we study God's Word, it is very easy to forget what we've learned over time. Since the lessons we learn from the Bible are so important, we don't want to forget them. Therefore, we want to study and memorize the Bible. Memorizing Bible verses will allow us to recall God's truths when we need them the most. We may need to recall God's Word as we make decisions, give advice to others, face challenges, fight against temptation, share our faith, etc.

Obey the Bible. James 1:22 states, "Do not merely listen to the word, and so deceive yourselves. Do what it says." Having knowledge of the Bible is a good start. Ultimately, God wants us to know the Bible and apply what we learn in our everyday lives. As we study the Bible, we can ask ourselves, "How can I implement what I just learned? Do I need to change my actions? Is there a good example in the Bible that I should follow? Is there a bad example in the Bible that I should avoid?" The lessons we learn from the Bible can be implemented in every aspect of our lives.

Share

- How often do you read and study God's Word? Make it a goal to start reading God's Word every day. Don't get discouraged if you miss a day. Keep trying!

- Describe a time when you learned a valuable lesson from God's Word and implemented it in your life. How did it make your life better?
- Identify at least one person in the Bible who set a bad example that you should avoid in your life.
- Read additional Bible verses: Psalm 119:4, 34, and 60.

Pray

Lord, fill my heart with a desire to study and memorize the Bible on a regular basis. Give me a deeper understanding of Your Word. Remind me that the Bible isn't just another book. I pray that I will obey Your Word at all times. Help me to implement Your Word in every area of my life. Amen.

Passion for Prayer

Do not be anxious about anything, but in every situation, by prayer and petition, with thanksgiving, present your requests to God.

Philippians 4:6

Tell God about It

Call to me and I will tell you great and
unsearchable things you do not know.

Jeremiah 33:3

Study

God wants to hear from us. We often feel comfortable sharing our thoughts with friends and family members. In addition, we should never forget to talk with God. Since God is our Father, He desires to hear from us. We can talk with God, because He actually cares. According to 1 Peter 5:7, we should, "Cast all your cares on Him because He cares for you." Knowing this, we should be eager to pray.

God cares about every aspect of our lives. Some people believe that God only cares about spiritual matters, such as Bible study, prayer, and church ministry. However, 1 Peter 5:7 reminds us to share "all" of our concerns with Him. God is concerned about every aspect of our lives. He wants to talk about our friends, school, health, family, good days, not-so-good days, and more. It is good to know that we can talk with God about anything!

The time and place doesn't matter to God. God is never too busy for us. We can talk with God at anytime and anyplace. Prayer is not limited to a certain place or a certain time of day. We can pray at home, school, work, and other places. Also, we can pray anytime during the day—morning, afternoon, or evening. God is available to speak with us at any time.

Share

- Do you feel that you can talk to God about anything? If not, why not?
- Do you feel comfortable talking to God anytime and anyplace? If not, why not?

Pray

Lord, thank You for the gift of prayer. I'm glad that I can talk with You about anything. I'm happy that I can talk with You anytime and anyplace. I'm glad that You are always available to talk with me. Thank You for caring about my life. Amen.

A Balanced Prayer Life—Praise

Great is the Lord and most worthy of praise.

Psalm 145:3

Study

In our prayers, it is easy to spend most of our time asking God to meet our personal needs. Instead, we should aim to have a balanced prayer life. One simple approach is called the ACTS model—adoration, confession, thanksgiving, and supplication.

God deserves the praise. During the adoration time of prayer, we praise God for all His wonderful qualities. Praise allows us to tell God how much we value and adore Him. Praising God can be tough, because it forces us to look beyond ourselves and focus entirely on Him. There are so many reasons to praise God. For example, God is self-sufficient, and He doesn't need our help (Acts 17:24–25). We can praise Him for His holiness (Psalm 99:5, 9); power (Psalm 147:5); wisdom (Romans 11:33–36); presence (Psalm 139:7–12); goodness (Psalm 135:3); and love (1 John 4:16). God is unique, and no one compares to Him (Isaiah 40:18, 46:9). Lastly, God is sovereign and free to do whatever He pleases (Psalm 135:6).

Give God our best praise. Whenever we praise God, we should do so with all our heart. Psalm 86:12 states, "I will praise you, Lord my God, with all my heart." Praising God isn't a short-term effort. We should praise God as long as we live. Psalm 63:4 states, "I will praise you as long as I live, and in your name I will lift up my hands."

Share

- Name at least two to three reasons to praise God.
- Read additional Bible verses: Psalms 115:3, 33:13–14 and Job 22:2.

Pray

Lord, You are worthy to be praised. No one compares to You. You have all wisdom and power. Your thoughts are higher than our thoughts. Your ways are higher than our ways. You are a holy God. You are a self-sufficient God who lacks nothing. I will glorify Your name forever. Nothing is too hard for You. I will praise You as long as I live. Amen.

A Balanced Prayer Life—Confession

If we confess our sins, He is faithful and just and will forgive
us our sins and purify us from all unrighteousness.

1 John 1:9

Study

Admit that we're wrong. During the confession time of prayer, we confess our sins to God. Confession allows us to agree with God concerning the sinful acts in our lives. Confessing our sins to God can be difficult, because we assume that we never do anything wrong. However, all of us have done something wrong. Romans 3:23 states, "For all have sinned and fall short of the glory of God." Even young children are capable of sinning. Psalm 51:5 states, "Surely I was sinful at birth, sinful from the time my mother conceived me." Therefore, confessing our sins is an important habit that we should embrace as early as possible.

Seek forgiveness and repentance. We serve a God who is willing to forgive us. As 1 John 1:9 reminds us, God will forgive us if we confess our sins to Him. Forgiveness allows us to make things right with God and move forward, despite our past mistakes. Repentance allows us to change our actions if we are doing something wrong. Psalm 119:59 states, "I have considered my ways and have turned my steps to your statutes." God doesn't want us to continue down the wrong path. Once we know the right thing to do, God expects us to do it.

Share

- Why is it so hard for people to confess their sins to God? Identify any sins that you have committed lately. Take the time to confess your sins privately to God, seek His forgiveness, and repent.
- Read additional Bible verses: Psalms 38:18; 51:2, 9; 66:18; 28:13; 32:5; and 1 John 3:6.

Pray

Lord, have mercy on me. I pray that You will forgive my sins. Create in me a pure heart. Cleanse me, and wash away my sins. Help me to repent and turn away from any words, thoughts, or actions that are not pleasing to You. Amen.

A Balanced Prayer Life—Thanksgiving

Let them give thanks to the Lord for his unfailing
love and his wonderful deeds for mankind.

Psalm 107:15

Study

During this time of prayer, we thank God for all the things He's done for us.

Thank God for all our blessings. We should thank God for *all* our blessings—not just the big things. Ephesians 5:20 states, "Always giving thanks to God the Father for everything, in the name of our Lord Jesus Christ." For example, we can thank God for giving us food, clothing, and shelter. We can thank Him for allowing us to have a good day at school or work. We can thank Him for surrounding us with positive people. We can thank God for His love, grace, forgiveness, guidance, and protection. The list of God's blessings goes on and on.

Don't forget about God after we receive the blessing. It is easy to assume that we've "earned" our blessings because of our skills and knowledge. We often forget that God is the true source of our blessings. James 1:17 states, "Every good and perfect gift comes from above, coming down from the Father of heavenly lights." Also, we can become so excited about our blessings that we forget to thank God. In Luke 17:11–19, ten men were healed of leprosy, but only one of them came back to thank God. Once we receive our blessings, we should never take God for granted. We should always thank God for all that He has done for us.

Share

- Name at least two to three things that you are thankful for.
- Read additional Bible verses: Colossians 4:2 and Psalms 100:4, 118:1.

Pray

Lord, thank You very much for everything that You do for me. You are a good God. All my blessings come from You. You are the true source of all my blessings. I pray that I will never take You for granted. Fill my heart with thanksgiving. Amen.

A Balanced Prayer Life—Supplication

Do not be anxious about anything, but in every situation, by prayer and petition, with thanksgiving, present your requests to God.

Philippians 4:6

Study

During this time of prayer, we pray for ourselves and others.

Praying for our own personal needs. Prayer demonstrates that we are dependent upon God to meet our needs. Philippians 4:19 states, "And my God will meet all your needs according to the riches of his glory in Christ Jesus." When we pray, we are telling God that we can't make it in life on our own, and we need His help. God is concerned about every aspect of our lives—school, work, health, relationships, family, money, etc. According to Philippians 4:6, we can present our requests to God in "every" situation. Also, Ephesians 6:18 reminds us to pray in the Spirit on "all" occasions.

Praying for the needs of others. Ephesians 6:18 encourages us to "keep on praying for all the Lord's people." Praying for others requires us to look beyond ourselves and consider the needs of others. Even in the midst of his difficult situation, Job prayed for his friends (Job 42:10). When Paul was in prison, the church prayed for him (Acts 12:1–5). Because we care about others, we want to see God make a difference in their lives too. Many people have been impacted in a positive way by the prayers of others. Prayer allows us to stand with others as they face life's challenges.

Share

- Identify at least two people that you can pray for. Contact those people, find out their prayer needs, and start praying for them this week.
- Read additional Bible verses: Philippians 1:3–4; Colossians 1:9; and 1 Thessalonians 1:2.

Pray

Lord, I'm so thankful that You are willing and able to meet my needs. I can't make it in life on my own. Help me to look beyond myself and pray for the needs of others. Amen.

Our Personal Devotional Time

Very early in the morning, while it was still dark, Jesus got up,
left the house and went off to a solitary place, where he prayed.
Simon and his companions went to look for him, and when they
found him, they exclaimed: "Everyone is looking for you!"

Mark 1:35–37

Study

Minimize the interruptions. During our devotional time, we set aside
time in our day to pray and study the Bible. In Mark 1:35, we see that
Jesus went to a quiet place to pray. However, in verse 37, Jesus was told,
"Everyone is looking for you!" Likewise, as soon as we decide to spend
time in prayer and Bible study, something will demand our attention. For
example, we may get interrupted by the noise of the television, telephone,
radio, or crying baby. It is very hard to pray and study the Bible when we
are distracted by so many things.

Monitor our busy schedule. In Mark 1:35–37, Jesus wanted to break away
from His busy schedule to spend time in prayer. Likewise, we shouldn't
become too busy to spend time in prayer and Bible study. Our schedules
are often filled with numerous activities—homework, band practice, soccer
practice, piano lessons, swimming lessons, work, and more. Even in the
process of doing good things, we don't want to ignore God. We should
always find time to pray and study the Bible.

Share

- How often do you pray and study the Bible? Is there anything that distracts you from praying and studying the Bible on a regular basis? If so, what can you do to minimize those distractions?
- Read additional Bible verses: Luke 5:16 and 10:38–41.

Pray

Lord, give me the desire to study the Bible and pray. Help me to minimize any distractions. I pray that I will never become too busy to pray and study the Bible. Amen.

Patience

Wait for the Lord; be strong and take heart and wait for the Lord.

Psalm 27:14

I Want It Now

Wait for the Lord; be strong and take heart and wait for the Lord.

Psalm 27:14

Study

We must learn to wait. We live in a fast-paced world where we want everything right now. We want to spend money and buy material things now. We don't like to wait in lines at stores or restaurants. It appears that the world moves too slowly when we're in a hurry to reach our destination. It can be tough to be patient at times. In the world of farming, a farmer must wait patiently to receive his crops. He realizes that it doesn't happen overnight. Likewise, we must learn how to be patient as well. We may not be able to receive everything we want in life overnight.

We must wait on God's plan. Although we have an idea of what we want in life, maybe God has something even better planned for us. Isaiah 48:17 reminds us that God knows what is best for us. If we want to receive God's best, then we must be willing to wait for His guidance (Psalm 5:3). If we fail to seek God's guidance, we may get what we want. However, we may not achieve the best results (Psalm 106:7–15). We must remember that rushing ahead of God can actually make things worse.

We must wait for the right time. Sometimes, we want the right things in life, but it's just not the right time to receive those things. Whenever we are in a hurry, we assume that God is taking too long to meet our needs. However, we must remember that God operates on His own timetable. God knows what is best for us, and He knows when it is best for us to have it. In the book of Genesis, Joseph had to wait years before he gained his ultimate leadership position. David had to wait years before he became the king. Waiting on God's timing can be tough, but it is worth it.

Share

- Discuss a time when you felt that God was moving too slowly for you. How did you react? Was it the best reaction?
- Read additional Bible verses: Psalm 46:10; Colossians 3:12; and Hebrews 6:13–15.

Pray

Lord, give me the patience to wait on You and trust Your timing. I realize that You know what is best for me, and You know when it is best for me to have it. Change my heart if I want something before it is time for me to have it. Bless me to be a person of patience. Amen.

Perseverance

Let perseverance finish its work so that you may be
mature and complete, not lacking anything.

James 1:4

Don't Give Up

Give careful thought to the paths for your feet
and be steadfast in all your ways.

Proverbs 4:26

Study

As we try to reach our goals in life, we may face obstacles along the way. Perseverance is our effort to keep moving forward when we are faced with obstacles in our path.

Perseverance helps us become better. Learning to persevere can help us grow and become better people. James 1:4 states, "Let perseverance finish its work so that you maybe mature and complete, not lacking anything." In Romans 5:3, we learn that perseverance builds our character. Whenever we are tempted to give up, we should surround ourselves with people who will encourage us to keep going. Also, we can think about others who didn't quit when they faced obstacles. For example, in the book of Genesis, we see that Joseph persevered and became a great leader of Egypt. He didn't quit when he was thrown into a pit and sent to prison.

Understand the consequences of quitting. There are so many reasons why we give up. For example, we lack the financial resources, confidence, or support needed to move forward. Also, we give up whenever we've tried so many times in the past to achieve our goal but didn't succeed. Whenever we face obstacles, giving up is often the quickest and easiest option to take. However, we want to know the impact of giving up. If we quit, what dreams or goals are we forfeiting? If others are depending on us, how will they be impacted if we fail to move forward? If we quit, are we missing out on an opportunity to grow spiritually? Although giving up can be the easiest thing to do, there are consequences.

Waiting on God is important too. In addition to perseverance, we must also learn to wait on God's timing. At the right time, God will allow us to reach those goals that He has approved. Of course, many of us believe that the right time is right now. We live in a world where we want everything right now. Many of us will give up if we can't reach our goals within our time frame. However, we must remember that God knows what is best for us.

Share

- Have you ever wanted to quit or give up on something? If so, please discuss. What inspired you to keep going and not quit?
- Read additional Bible verse: Hebrews 12:1–2.

Pray

Lord, give me the strength and wisdom to keep moving forward when I face obstacles. Help me to stay on track and never lose sight of Your plan for my life. I pray that You will use obstacles to build me up and not tear me down. Teach me how to persevere so that I can grow and become a better person. Build my character as I learn to persevere. Surround me with the right people who will encourage me to keep going. Whenever I feel like quitting, help me to keep my eyes focused on Jesus, who never quit even when He died on the cross for me. Amen.

Purity

But among you there must not be even a hint of sexual immorality, or of any kind of impurity, or of greed, because these are improper for God's holy people.

Ephesians 5:3

The Hidden Truths about Sex—Part 1

Do you not know that your bodies are temples of the Holy Spirit, who is in you, whom you have received from God? You are not your own; you were bought at a price. Therefore honor God with your bodies.

1 Corinthians 6:19–20

Study

Sex is a gift from God. Sex is a gift from God. It is designed for a man and woman who are in a committed marriage that glorifies Him. Sexual union is God's plan to initiate physical and emotional unity in marriage. Genesis 2:24 states, "For this reason a man will leave his father and mother and be united to his wife, and they will become one flesh." Also, God created sex to allow us to bear children who will expand His image here on earth. Genesis 1:28 states, "God blessed them and said to them, 'Be fruitful and increase in number; fill the earth and subdue it.'" Since God is the creator of sex, we should consult Him concerning how sex should be used. He knows what's best for us, because He created sex.

Our bodies belong to God. Society teaches us that it is okay to have sex as long as both participants consent to do so. Many people believe that we can do whatever we please with our bodies. As Christians, we must do whatever pleases God. We believe that our bodies belong to Him. First Corinthians 6:13 states, "The body, however, is not meant for sexual immorality but for the Lord, and the Lord for the body." God wants us to honor Him with our bodies. It is His will for us to live a life of purity. First Thessalonians 4:3 states, "It is God's will that you should be sanctified: that you should avoid sexual immorality."

Sex can hurt our fellowship with God. Whenever we use sex in a sinful way, it hurts our fellowship with God. First Thessalonians 4:7–8 states, "For God did not call us to be impure, but to live a holy life. Therefore, anyone who rejects this instruction does not reject a human being but God, the very God who gives you his Holy Spirit." Furthermore, whenever we encourage other people to commit sexual sin with us, it hurts their fellowship with God too. As 1 Thessalonians 4:6 states, "And that in this matter no one should wrong or take advantage of a brother or sister." We never want to be a stumbling block for others. Our actions should drive people closer to God, not push them further away.

Share

- Do you believe that we have the right to do whatever we please with our bodies? Why or why not?
- How does it feel to know that our sexual activity can impact our fellowship with God?

Prayer

Lord, I believe that my body belongs to You. Help me to only use my body in a way that is pleasing to You. Since You are the creator of sex, You know what is best for me. Enable me to live a life of purity and stay away from sexual sin. Amen.

The Hidden Truths about Sex—Part 2

See to it that no one takes you captive through hollow and
deceptive philosophy, which depends on human tradition and
the basic principles of this world rather than on Christ.

Colossians 2:8

Study

Sex doesn't guarantee a serious commitment. After two people have sex,
one person may assume that a serious relationship will be the next step.
However, the other person may not feel the same way. At that point, we
learn that two people can have casual sex and not be seriously committed
to each other. The world teaches us that it is okay to have sex first and then
hope that it will lead to a serious commitment later. However, we should
first make the serious commitment of marriage and then sex should follow.

Sex doesn't guarantee love. We shouldn't feel pressured to have sex to
demonstrate our love for another person. One person will say to the other
person, "If you really loved me, you would have sex with me." We shouldn't
assume that people love us because they have sex with us. It is possible for
two people to have sex and not love each other. If we love each other, we
should be willing to wait for marriage to have sex.

Sex can lead to guilt. Many people regret their decision to have sex before
marriage. Once we've been exposed to the truth in God's Word, the act
of sex can lead to guilty feelings. After the sex is over, we don't feel good
about it, because we've done something that wasn't pleasing to God. As a
result, we may despise the other person or distance ourselves from him or
her. We wrongfully assumed that the act of sex would draw us closer to

the other person. However, when sex is done outside of God's will, it can actually push two people apart.

Sex can lead to teen pregnancy. Sex before marriage can lead to unplanned pregnancies. With their new responsibilities as young mothers, many young girls find it difficult to complete their high school education. Research indicates that only 40 percent of teen mothers finish high school, and less than 2 percent of those who have a child before the age of eighteen will finish college by the age of thirty.[16] In some cases, the young girls are left to parent their children by themselves.

Sex can lead to disease. Having sex before marriage opens up the door to unwanted diseases. Unfortunately, sexually transmitted diseases (STDs) have become common among teens. Many people believe that getting a disease could "never happen to them." However, some people with STDs are probably unaware that they even have a disease. People can easily pass on STDs to others without even knowing it.

Share

- Do you believe that it's okay to have sex with someone if you love that person? Why or why not?
- Do you believe that it's okay to try out sex with someone before you marry him or her? Why or why not?
- Make a commitment to save the act of sex for marriage.

Prayer

Lord, thank You for teaching me the truth about sex through Your Word. Protect me from being deceived by our culture. Give me discernment so that I will know the difference between right and wrong. Bless me with the wisdom to always follow what's right. I know that the enemy wants to hide the truth from me. As I'm exposed to our culture's message about sex, remind me of the consequences that people fail to mention. Amen.

Know the Solutions—Part 1

No temptation has overtaken you except what is common to mankind. And God is faithful; he will not let you be tempted beyond what you can bear. But when you are tempted, he will also provide a way out so that you can endure it.

1 Corinthians 10:13

Study

Whenever we face temptation, we must know that God will show us a way out. However, we must be willing to take it. Very often, we know that we can escape the temptation, but we don't have the desire to do so.

Monitor our eyes. Job 31:1 states, "I made a covenant with my eyes not to look lustfully at a young woman." In Matthew 5:27–28, we learn that sin often starts with the eyes. At an early age, many males are taught to stare at females in a lustful way and have impure thoughts about them. In 2 Samuel 11:1–26, we learn that David's sin with Bathsheba started with a look of lust. After David looked at Bathsheba the first time, he could have walked away. However, he didn't. An attractive person may catch our eye the first time, but it should stop there. If we're not careful, the first look may evolve into multiple looks and then ungodly actions.

Monitor our thoughts. Sin often starts in our minds. We don't want to find ourselves thinking about another person in a sinful way. Although there is no physical contact, we can become emotionally attached to another person. Impure thoughts can build up an appetite to be with another person physically. Even our thoughts can't be hidden from God. He knows what we're thinking. Impure thoughts can lead to impure actions. If we're not careful, we may "act out" our ungodly thoughts.

Therefore, it is important to be transformed by the renewal of our minds (Romans 12:1–2). Also, Philippians 4:8 reminds us to focus our minds on pure thoughts.

Be careful with our media choices. Unfortunately, inappropriate sexual content is integrated into almost every form of media. While searching the Internet, we are exposed to sexual images for free. As we watch TV and movies, we see people engaged in sexual activity that goes against God's original plan. While reading magazines, we receive tips on how to "improve" our sexual activities with others. If we become overexposed to such content, we may let our guard down and embrace ungodly messages. As soon as we are exposed to ungodly content, we should immediately "flee" from the situation (1 Corinthians 6:18).

Stay away from pornography. Pornography is any form of media that is used to generate sexual excitement—magazines, movies, television, the Internet, etc. It typically includes images of naked people and/or people having sex with one another. It can encourage us to have lustful desires. Pornography sends a message that women are sex objects who are always ready to have sex. It also sends a message that it is okay to have casual sex with total strangers.

Share

- What steps can you take to protect yourself from looking at another person in a lustful way?
- Make a commitment to only support media choices that are good for you.
- Parents: Purchase special software to minimize your child's exposure to inappropriate material on the computer.
- Parents: Review good websites to learn about the appropriateness of content in popular movies. Try www.pluggedin.com and www .parentpreviews.com.

Pray

Lord, help me to never look at another person in a lustful way. Enable me to only use my eyes in a manner that is pleasing to You. Help me to discern the content that enters into my heart and mind through TV, movies, the Internet, and other media outlets. Enable me to renew my mind on a daily basis through Your Word. Protect me from thinking about another person in a lustful way. Keep my mind focused on pure thoughts. Amen.

Know the Solutions—Part 2

How can a young person stay on the path of
purity? By living according to your word.

Psalm 119:9

Study

Pursue a lifestyle of abstinence. God wants us to save sex for the right
time, which is marriage. Many people feel pressured to have sex, because
everyone else is doing it. Abstinence requires us to refrain from those
behaviors that involve sexual sin. The world wants us to believe that
abstinence is outdated. However, abstinence allows us to please God in
our relationships. It allows us to see that we can be in a good relationship
without being sexually involved. Abstinence may be tough, but it is worth it.

Seek accountability. Ecclesiastics 4:9–10 states, "Two are better than
one, because they have a good return for their labor: If either of them falls
down, one can help the other up." It is much harder to win the purity battle
when we're isolated from the right people. We need to surround ourselves
with other people who can encourage us, pray for us, and ask the tough
questions.

Set boundaries and expectations. We need to be up front and
communicate our expectations about sex in a relationship. We should
define boundaries that will keep us out of trouble (e.g., no spending the
night, ungodly movies/TV shows, secrecy dating, foreplay, flirting, etc.).
We should be very careful about entering relationships with people who
don't view sex from God's perspective. Through persistence, the other
person may "wear us down" and convince us to "give in" to sex. If we
must choose between our relationship with God and our relationship with

someone else, our relationship with God should be our top priority. We don't need to compromise our values to be in a relationship with another person.

Watch our clothing. Many females feel pressured to dress in a very suggestive manner—short, short skirts, short shorts, tight-fitting clothing, low-cut tops, etc. We want our young girls to be treated with respect and dignity. Therefore, modesty is a good approach for clothing.

Share

- Start practicing abstinence today. It is never too late to get started. Regardless of your past actions, you can get a fresh start today.
- Advance preparation is important. Write down those key boundaries you want to establish up front in your relationships with the opposite sex. Stick to your boundaries, and don't compromise.
- Identify at least one person who can help keep you accountable in the area of purity. Contact this person this week to see if he or she will be your accountability partner.

Pray

Lord, equip me with the discipline to save sex for marriage. Protect me from giving into sex because everybody else is doing it. Surround me with godly people who can hold me accountable. Encourage me to set up boundaries that will keep me out of trouble in this area of my life. I pray that I will never become a stumbling block to others with my clothing. Keep me away from those people who encourage me to disobey You. My relationship with You, Lord, is my top priority. Amen.

Know the Solutions—Part 3

But among you there must not be even a hint of sexual
immorality, or of any kind of impurity, or of greed,
because these are improper for God's holy people.

Ephesians 5:3

Study

We should pray and study the Word of God. Psalm 119:9 states, "How
can a young person stay on the path of purity? By living according to your
word." For example, the Bible is filled with practical advice about purity.
Obeying God's Word will keep us on the right track and help us avoid sin.
Psalm 119:11 states, "I have hidden your word in my heart that I might
not sin against you." Hiding God's Word in our hearts will help us to be
prepared to fight and win against temptation when it comes. In addition,
we should rely on prayer to help us remain pure. Matthew 26:41 states,
"Watch and pray so that you will not fall into temptation. The spirit is
willing, but the flesh is weak." Prayer demonstrates that we are dependent
upon God to help us live a life of purity.

Watch out for foreplay. Foreplay describes those activities that can lead to
sex—excessive kissing, touching, rubbing, flirting, etc. We assume that we
can "play with fire" without getting burned. On the surface, these actions
appear to be innocent. One person will say to the other, "At least we're
not having sex. We're not doing anything wrong." However, foreplay can
lead to sex if we're not careful. Avoiding the act of sex is great. In addition,
we should avoid any activity that even leads us down the pathway to sex.

Escape the situation. In Genesis 39:6–12, we see a practical example of
how to deal with temptation. When Joseph was approached by Potiphar's

wife with an offer of sexual sin, he fled the situation. Likewise, if we ever find ourselves faced with temptation, we also need to flee the situation. First Corinthians 6:18 states, "Flee from sexual immorality." If we remain in the situation, we may "give in" to the temptation. We shouldn't hang around and hope that things will get better. Escaping the situation will allow us to see things more clearly and avoid the consequences of giving into temptation.

Share

- What would you do if someone wanted you to participate in foreplay? Have a game plan in place now. Don't wait until the time comes.
- Make a commitment to study God's Word and pray about your purity.

Pray

Lord, help me to resist any activity that leads to sexual sin. Encourage me to embrace modesty as I choose my clothing. Keep me away from pornography and all ungodly material at all times. Whenever I am faced with temptation, give me the wisdom and strength to flee the situation. Enable me to hide Your Word in my heart so that I don't sin against You. Remind me to pray and seek Your help concerning this area of my life. Amen.

Role Model

Join together in following my example, brothers and sisters,
and just as you have us as a model, keep your
eyes on those who live as we do.

Philippians 3:17

Be a Good Example for Others

Follow my example, as I follow the example of Christ.

1 Corinthians 11:1

Study

Seek to be good examples for others to follow. A role model is a person whose behavior is imitated by others. Therefore, a role model is someone who influences the behavior of others. As Christians, people will pay close attention to the way we act, think, speak, dress, treat others, etc. God wants us to have a positive influence on those around us. Matthew 5:13 states, "You are the salt of the earth." Whenever salt comes in contact with food, it makes the food better. Likewise, God wants His people to be a positive influence and make the world a better place. In Philippians 3:17, Paul spoke to the people and said, "Join together in following my example, brothers and sisters, and just as you have us as a model, keep your eyes on those who live as we do."

We can set good examples at all ages. Regardless of our age, each one of us can be a good influence on others. In the book of Timothy, we learn about Timothy who was a young pastor. Although he was young, he set a good example for others to follow. In 1 Timothy 4:12, we are counseled: "Don't let anyone look down on you because you are young, but set an example for the believers in speech, in conduct, in love, in faith and in purity." Therefore, even young people can serve as good role models.

Our lives should point people to Christ. As other people observe our lifestyles, they should be encouraged to live for Christ. In 1 Corinthians 11:1, Paul encouraged the people to follow his example as he followed the example of Christ. Likewise, people should observe our lifestyles and be encouraged to follow Christ. In Matthew 5:14, we are called to be the "light of the world." As the light of the world, we want our lives to ultimately point people to Jesus Christ.

Share

- Identify two to three ways that you can be a positive influence on others.

Pray

Lord, help me to be the salt of the earth and have a positive influence on those around me. Remind me that others are always observing my behavior as a Christian. Equip me to be a person who always sets a godly example for others to follow. Equip me to be the light of the world so that my life will always point others to Jesus Christ. Amen.

Follow the Right Examples

I have set you an example that you should do as I have done for you.

John 13:15

Study

Know the influencers. A study of teenagers was conducted to identify people they admire most (besides their parents). The study revealed that teenagers are most likely to admire other family members and then teachers, coaches, friends, and pastors.[17] Beyond those people they know personally, young people also admire sports heroes, political leaders, business leaders, medical professionals, and members of the military.[18]

Be aware of other people's intentions. The study revealed that teenagers are most likely to admire people who encourage them, make them feel good about themselves, and show an interest in their future.[19] First Thessalonians 5:11 reminds us to "encourage one another and build each other up." It is easy to be drawn to people who show an interest in our lives. However, we must protect ourselves from people who may want to harm us. As we pray, we should ask God to surround us with people who have the right motives.

Follow the right behavior. Sometimes, a person will demonstrate success in one area of his or her life but does not please God in other areas. Therefore, it is possible to admire others for their successes without actually embracing their ungodly behaviors. For example, a bright student may do well in the classroom but still not live for God. Even as we select role models, we never want to follow any behavior that isn't pleasing to God. As Christians, we aspire to be like Jesus Christ, who is our ultimate role model. As we pray, God can help us know the difference between right and wrong. As we strive to live for Christ, we can follow the positive examples set by others who are also living for Christ.

Share

- Identify at least two people you admire the most. What exactly do you admire about them?
- Have you ever followed the wrong behavior of someone else? If so, please explain.

Pray

Lord, I aspire to live like Jesus Christ, who is our ultimate role model. As I live for You, God, surround me with people who are also living for You. Give me discernment so that I will know the difference between right and wrong. Help me to only live out those actions that are pleasing to You. Protect me from people who may want to harm me. Give me the desire to please You at all times. Amen.

Salvation

For God so loved the world that He gave his one and only Son, that whoever believes in Him shall not perish but have eternal life.

John 3:16

Salvation

For God so loved the world that He gave his one and only Son, that
whoever believes in Him shall not perish but have eternal life.

John 3:16

Study

Salvation is available to all. According to 1 Timothy 2:3–4, "This is
good, and pleases God our Savior, who wants all people to be saved and
to come to a knowledge of the truth." God offers the gift of eternal life
to everyone regardless of their education, race, financial wealth, family
background, political affiliation, geographical location, etc. Acts 2:21
states, "And everyone who calls on the name of the Lord will be saved."
God desires to see all of us spend eternity with Him. John 6:40 states, "For
my Father's will is that everyone who looks to the Son and believes in Him
shall have eternal life." Eternal life is available to all of us.

Jesus Christ is the only way. Acts 4:12 states, "Salvation is found in no one
else, for there is no other name under heaven given to mankind by which
we must be saved." The world teaches us that there are many different ways
to experience salvation. As Christians, we believe that Jesus Christ is the
only way to experience salvation. John 3:36 states, "Whoever believes in
the Son has eternal life." John 10:9 states, "I am the gate; whoever enters
through me will be saved."

We can't earn our salvation. Ephesians 2:8–9 states, "For it is by grace
you have been saved, through faith—and this is not from yourselves, it is
the gift of God—not by works, so that no one can boast." Salvation is only
made possible by God's grace. It is a gift from God to us. We didn't earn
it or deserve it. We can't earn salvation through our own human efforts.

John 1:12–13 reminds us that God is the one who makes it possible for us to become members of His family. God deserves all the glory for the gift of our salvation.

Share

- What are the different ways that people may try to "earn" salvation on their own?
- Read additional Bible verses: 1 Corinthians 15:1–8; John 3:1–7, 5:24, 5:39–40; and Ephesians 2:11–13.

Pray

Lord, thank You so much for the gift of eternal life. I believe that trusting in Jesus Christ as our Lord and Savior is the only way to experience salvation. I know that I can't earn my salvation. It is only by Your grace that we have access to eternal life. Thank You for offering the gift of eternal life to all people. Amen.

Becoming a Christian

For God so loved the world that He gave his one and only Son,
that whoever believes in Him shall not perish but have eternal life.

John 3:16

Study

Becoming a Christian is the most important decision that we can make in our lifetime. God loves us, and He wants us to have a personal relationship with Him forever. In becoming Christians, we want to admit that we are sinners; we believe that Jesus Christ died for our sins; we repent and turn away from our sins; and we trust in Jesus Christ alone as our Savior.

All of us have sinned. Romans 3:23 states, "For all have sinned and fall short of the glory of God." Although God wants us to have a personal relationship with Him forever, our personal sin separates us from Him. Sin takes place whenever we decide to disobey God. All of us have done something wrong at some point in our lives.

The penalty for sin is eternal separation from God. Romans 6:23 states, "For the wages of sin is death, but the gift of God is eternal life in Christ Jesus our Lord." Here is the bad news: our sin creates a big gap between God and us. Because of our sin, we deserve to be separated from God forever.

Jesus paid the price for our sins on the cross. Here is the good news. Romans 5:8 states, "But God demonstrates his own love for us in this: While we were still sinners, Christ died for us." When Jesus Christ died on the cross, He paid the penalty for our sins. Through His death, Jesus bridged the gap between God and us. God raised Jesus from the dead to overcome sin.

We can trust in Him as our Savior. Romans 10:9 states, "That if you confess with your mouth, 'Jesus is Lord,' and believe in your heart that God raised him from the dead, you will be saved." Jesus did His part by dying for us on the cross. Now, we must do our part by trusting in Him alone as our Savior.

Share

Becoming a Christian is only the starting point of our exciting journey with God. Once we become Christians, we must continue to grow in our relationship with Jesus Christ. Here are some practical steps to take:

- Get baptized to publicly profess your faith to others.
- Pray and read your Bible on a daily basis to get to know Christ better.
- Share your faith by telling others about Jesus Christ.
- Join a Bible-teaching church where Jesus Christ is preached and where you can worship, serve, and fellowship with other Christians.

Pray

Would you like to tell God that you want to trust in Jesus Christ alone as your Savior? If so, please tell Him by praying the following prayer:

Lord, I know that I'm a sinner. I know that my sin separates me from You. Please forgive my sins. I believe that Jesus Christ died for my sins and rose from the dead. I ask You to come into my life today. I trust Jesus Christ alone as my Lord and Savior. In Jesus's name I pray. Amen.

Servant's Heart

When the ten heard about this, they became indignant with James and John. Jesus called them together and said, "You know that those who are regarded as rulers of the Gentiles lord it over them, and their high officials exercise authority over them. Not so with you. Instead, whoever wants to become great among you must be your servant, and whoever wants to be first must be slave of all. For even the Son of Man did not come to be served, but to serve, and to give his life as a ransom for many.

Mark 10:41–45

Get Involved Today

Then he said to his disciples,
"The harvest is plentiful but the workers are few.
Ask the Lord of the harvest, therefore,
to send out workers into his harvest field."

Matthew 9:37–38

Study

Our gifts are needed. In Matthew 9:37–38, we learn that those who serve the Lord can be few. It is believed that 80 percent of ministry activities are done by 20 percent of the church members. Every single member of God's family is needed to serve. Some people are comfortable just going to church on Sunday mornings. However, a Sunday morning experience is not enough. God also wants us to use our talents and abilities to serve others.

Stay focused on God's plan for you. God blesses each of His children with different spiritual gifts to serve Him in different ways. God is able to give us exactly what we need to serve the people He's calling us to reach. Although God has given us different gifts, we still have one thing in common—we serve the same God. Our relationship with Christ is the central link that ties us together, regardless of our spiritual gifts. God is the provider and enabler of our gifts.

Ensure that God receives the glory. We should never use our spiritual gifts to glorify ourselves. As we observe how God is using our gifts to bless others, we shouldn't become arrogant. It is only by God's grace that we have spiritual gifts. Whenever we serve others, we want to point people toward Jesus Christ so that He may receive the glory.

Share

- How exactly are you using your abilities to serve others? If you're not serving others, find a church ministry where you can serve.

Pray

Lord, I know that the harvest is plentiful but the workers are few. Send me out to be one of Your servants. Help me to be a great team player. Show me how I can get involved in ministry. I pray that You will receive all the glory when I serve others. Amen.

Follow the Example of Christ

When the ten heard about this, they became indignant with James and John. Jesus called them together and said, "You know that those who are regarded as rulers of the Gentiles lord it over them, and their high officials exercise authority over them. Not so with you. Instead, whoever wants to become great among you must be your servant, and whoever wants to be first must be slave of all. For even the Son of Man did not come to be served, but to serve, and to give his life as a ransom for many.

Mark 10:41–45

Study

Focus on the needs of others. When it comes to serving others, we should adopt the attitude of Jesus Christ. He came to earth to serve others. Mark 10:45 states, "For even the Son of Man did not come to be serve, but to serve." God calls us to look beyond ourselves and meet the needs of others. Philippians 2:3 states, "Each of you should look not only to your own interests, but also to the interests of others." Life can be very rewarding when we know that we're meeting the needs of others.

Adopt a new view of greatness. In Mark 10, we learn that James and John sought high positions and status in Jesus's kingdom. The world teaches us that greatness is determined by how many people serve us. Some people are more willing to serve in a ministry if they can be leaders. However, Jesus taught that our greatness comes from serving others. In Mark 10:43, it states, "Not so with you. Instead, whoever wants to become great among you must be your servant." As Christians, we believe that greatness is found in serving others.

Serve others regardless of the task. With a servant's heart, we are willing to serve God regardless of the size of the task. Some people are only willing to serve God when there is a big task involved. We should never assume that certain tasks are below us. Great opportunities often show up in small tasks. When Jesus washed the feet of His disciples, He chose a task that was reserved for household servants. Despite His status, Jesus was willing to perform the task anyway. In Philippians 2:7, we are reminded that Jesus embraced His role as a servant. If Jesus was willing to perform unglamorous tasks then surely we should be able to do the same.

Share

- Have you ever believed that greatness only comes from being at the top and being served by others? If so, what factors influenced you to think that way?
- Is it hard for you to look beyond yourself and meet the needs of others? If so, please explain.
- Have you ever believed that certain tasks were beneath you? If so, what made you feel that way?

Pray

Lord, thank You for being an excellent example of a true servant. Despite Your status, You came to earth to serve others. Because of Your example, I want to go and serve others. Remove any selfishness from my heart. Help me to look beyond myself and meet the needs of others. Help me to realize that greatness comes from serving others. Amen.

Sharing Our Faith

But you will receive power when the Holy Spirit comes on you; and you will be my witnesses in Jerusalem, and in all Judea and Samaria, and to the ends of the earth.

Acts 1:8

Sharing Our Faith

Then Jesus came to them and said, "All authority in heaven and on earth
has been given to me. Therefore go and make disciples of all nations,
baptizing them in the name of the Father and of the Son and of the
Holy Spirit, and teaching them to obey everything I have commanded
you. And surely I am with you always, to the very end of the age."

Matthew 28:18–20

Study

We're all needed. In fulfilling the Great Commission, God calls all of us
to "go and make disciples of all nations." However, many Christians are
hesitant to share their faith. Matthew 9:37 says, "The harvest is plentiful
but the workers are few." The world is filled with a harvest of people who
need to trust in Jesus Christ alone as their Savior. However, we must have
the courage to share our faith with them. It is easy to assume that sharing
our faith is only reserved for pastors and full-time missionaries. However,
God expects all His followers to get involved.

We're partners with God. God could have chosen any method to deliver
the Gospel message to the world. However, He chose to use His people. We
have been given the privilege to partner with God in spreading the Gospel
message. We play a key role in reaching people for Christ. It is truly an
honor that God entrusts us with the Gospel message. First Thessalonians
2:4 states, "On the contrary, we speak as those approved by God to be
entrusted with the gospel."

Sharing our faith is critical. Once we become Christians, it is easy to
forget that other people need to trust in Christ as their Savior too. We
shouldn't say to ourselves, "Now that I have a personal relationship with

Christ, I'll let other people worry about their own relationship with Him." We shouldn't keep the Gospel message to ourselves. We must remember that another person's eternal destiny is on the line. God desires to change that destiny from eternal death to eternal life. In Romans 10:14, we are reminded that people can't take advantage of the gift of eternal life if they never hear the Gospel.

Share

- Make a commitment to share your faith with others on a regular basis. Share your faith with at least one person this month.
- Pray that God will allow you to cross paths with people who need to hear the Gospel message.

Pray

Lord, give me the desire to share my faith with others. Help me to look beyond myself and realize that others need to trust in Jesus Christ as their Lord and Savior. Remind me that the Great Commission is for all of us— not just a select few. Thank You for the privilege and honor to share Your Gospel message with others. Help me to overcome my fears about sharing my faith. Remind me that someone else's eternal destiny is on the line. Give me the courage and boldness to be Your witness. Amen.

Stress

Cast all your anxiety on him because he cares for you.

1 Peter 5:7

Stressing Out—Part 1

Who of you by worrying can add a single hour to your life?

Matthew 6:27

Study

Know the consequences. When the pressures of life become too much, we often feel stressed. People experience stress for various reasons—homework, exams, relationships, problems with peers, family, health, and a busy schedule. Worrying about our situation can only make it worse. Stress can lead to many illnesses, affect our mood, and cause us to lose sleep at night.

Talk to God about it. During our times of stress, God doesn't want us to face the problems of life by ourselves. We can talk to God, because He cares about our problems (1 Peter 5:7). Instead of worrying about our situation, God wants us to pray about it. As we pray, God is able to give us peace so that we can make it through our stressful situation. Once we ask God to help us with our problems, we must believe that He can work it out for us. The pressures of life are difficult for us, but nothing is too hard for God (Jeremiah 32:27).

Find healthy ways to deal with stress. Some people respond to stress in unhealthy ways by turning to drugs, alcohol, and unhealthy eating. In addition to prayer, we can also respond to stress with rest, exercise, fun activities, and surrounding ourselves with positive people. We can also take a look at our schedule and determine which activities need to stay and which need to be removed. In Luke 5:15–16, Jesus teaches us the importance of saying no to a busy schedule.

Share

- How do you typically respond to the stressful situations of life?
- Does worrying make your situation better or worse?
- Identify at least two techniques that you can use to overcome stress.

Pray

Lord, protect me from being overwhelmed by the pressures of life. Encourage me to pray about my situation instead of worrying about it. As I pray, bless me with Your peace. Guard my heart and mind against all stress and worry. Bless me to have total trust and confidence in Your ability to handle my situation. Remind me that worrying is more harmful than helpful. Help me to keep a balanced life and say no when needed. Show me how to respond to the demands of life in a manner that is pleasing to You. Amen.

Thoughts

Do not conform to the pattern of this world, but be transformed by the renewing of your mind. Then you will be able to test and approve what God's will is—his good, pleasing and perfect will.

Romans 12:2

Good Thoughts

Finally, brothers and sisters, whatever is true, whatever is noble, whatever is right, whatever is pure, whatever is lovely, whatever is admirable—if anything is excellent or praiseworthy—think about such things.

Philippians 4:8

Study

Think good thoughts. In Philippians 4:8, Paul encourages us to focus our minds on good thoughts. Reading God's Word is a great way to fill our minds with good thoughts. God's Word is a filter to help us keep the good thoughts and get rid of any bad thoughts. In John 8:44, we learn that our enemy is the "father of lies." He wants to fill our minds with thoughts of doubt, fear, worry, low self-esteem, hate, violence, impurity, etc. However, there is good news. We aren't required to accept every thought that crosses our mind. God has given us the power to say no to any thoughts that aren't pleasing to Him.

Monitor our media intake. On a daily basis, we are exposed to many messages through television, the Internet, magazines, movies, and radio. Therefore, we should monitor our media choices and stay away from any content that isn't pleasing to God. If we feel uncomfortable with the content, we have the power to turn off the music, turn to another TV channel, read a different magazine, and visit another website.

Our thoughts help determine our actions. In Philippians 4:9, it states, "Whatever you have learned or received or heard from me, or seen in me—put it into practice." Our actions usually begin with a thought. Godly thoughts lead to godly actions, and negative thoughts can lead to negative actions.

Share

- Whenever you are exposed to negative messages, find a way to block those messages or remove yourself from the situation. Think about your game plan in advance, and be prepared.

Pray

Lord, fill my mind with thoughts that are true, noble, right, pure, lovely, admirable, excellent, and praiseworthy. Help me to choose my thoughts wisely. Help me to say yes to the right thoughts and no to the wrong thoughts. Amen.

Wisdom

For the Lord gives wisdom; from his mouth
come knowledge and understanding.

Proverbs 2:6

Seeking Wisdom

If any of you lacks wisdom, you should ask God, who gives
generously to all without finding fault, and it will be given to you.

James 1:5

Study

Wisdom requires obedience. The world teaches us that people are considered
wise based on their education and intelligence. However, people become
wise by listening to God and following His instructions. Wisdom requires
us to know what's right and actually do it. Matthew 7:24 states, "Therefore
everyone who hears these words of mine and puts them into practice is like
a wise man who built his house on the rock."

Wisdom leads us down the right path. If we follow God's guidance, then
He will lead us in the right direction. Isaiah 48:17–18 reminds us, "I am
the Lord your God, who teaches you what is best for you, who directs you
in the way you should go." Proverbs 4:11 states, "I instruct you in the way
of wisdom and lead you along straight paths."

Seek wise counsel. God is willing to share wisdom with those who are
willing to seek it. We can always turn to God as our ultimate source of
wisdom. We can use prayer and Bible study as tools to tap into God's
wisdom. Proverbs 2:6 states, "For the Lord gives wisdom; from his mouth
come knowledge and understanding." Additional insight can also be
obtained from other key people, such as parents, family members, mentors,
and godly friends. Proverbs 13:20 states, "Walk with the wise and become
wise."

Share

- Describe a time when you used wisdom to follow the right path in life.
- Do you have access to godly people who can share wise counsel with you? If not, what can you do to get connected to the right people?
- Read additional Bible verses: Proverbs 9:9, 12; 2:1–15; 3:13–18; and Ephesians 5:15.

Pray

Lord, I know that You are the ultimate source of wisdom. Lead me down the right path in life. Teach me what is best for me. Equip me with wisdom so that I can do what's right at all times. Surround me with godly people who can share wise counsel with me. Amen.

Worth

Are not five sparrows sold for two pennies? Yet not one of them is forgotten by God. Indeed, the very hairs of your head are all numbered. Don't be afraid; you are worth more than many sparrows.

Luke 12:6–7

We Are Valuable to God

For you created my inmost being; you knit me together in my mother's womb. I praise you because I am fearfully and wonderfully made; your works are wonderful, I know that full well.

Psalm 139:13–14

Study

Our value isn't determined by others. Sometimes, we don't feel valued as a person because of our education, race, gender, physical appearance, family background, and other factors. Many girls only feel valuable if someone else thinks that they are pretty or have the "right" body shape. Likewise, many boys only feel valued if they play sports very well. Some young people often feel more valued when they hang out with the "cool" crowd. We live in a world that is constantly telling us that we're not good enough. However, God thinks differently. We are valuable in His eyes.

We should focus on what God thinks about us. We are valuable, because we are created by God. Ephesians 2:10 states, "We are God's workmanship." God sees us as His masterpiece. A masterpiece is considered to be a person's greatest piece of work. Furthermore, God considers us to be the "apple" of His eye. Psalm 17:8 states, "Keep me as the apple of your eye." Additionally, God sees value in us, because He allowed His only Son to die on the cross on our behalf (John 3:16). Therefore, we shouldn't allow other people to determine our personal value.

Share

- Do you believe that you are valuable and significant? Why or why not?
- Has anyone ever made you feel as if you aren't valuable? If so, explain.
- Read additional Bible verses: 1 Peter 2:9 and Luke 12:6–7.

Pray

Lord, enable me to see myself from Your perspective. I believe that my value is determined by You. Thank You for being my Creator and seeing me as Your masterpiece. Remind me on a daily basis that I am wonderfully made by You. I am Your workmanship. Help me to drown out any voices that say I'm not valuable because of my race, gender, physical appearance, or any other factor. Keep me as the apple of Your eye. Amen.

About the Author

William Rollings is on a mission to encourage and equip people to reach their God-given potential. He is the also the author of *Jump-Start Your Day*. He and his lovely wife, Grenna, have two beautiful daughters, Alexis and Alyssa. For more information, please visit his website at www .williamrollings.com.

References

1   D. K. Eaton, L. Kann, and S. Kinchen, "Youth Risk Behavior
     Surveillance—United States, 2011," *CDC Morbidity and Mortality
     Weekly Report* (2012), accessed May 19, 2014. http://www.cdc.gov/
     mmwr/preview/mmwrhtml/ss6104a1.htm.

2   Dove. "The Real Truth About Beauty: Revisited." Accessed May 19,
     2014. http://www.dove.us/Social-Mission/Self-Esteem-Statistics.aspx.

3   D. K. Eaton, L. Kann, and S. Kinchen, "Youth Risk Behavior
     Surveillance—United States, 2011," *CDC Morbidity and Mortality
     Weekly Report* (2012), accessed May 19, 2014. http://www.cdc.gov/
     mmwr/preview/mmwrhtml/ss6104a1.htm.

4   National Highway Traffic Safety Administration. "Traffic Safety
     Facts 2012 Data: Young Drivers." Accessed May 19, 2014. http://
     www-nrd.nhtsa.dot.gov/Pubs/812019.pdf.

5   Centers for Disease Control. "Fact Sheets—Underage Drinking."
     Accessed May 19, 2014. http://www.cdc.gov/alcohol/fact-sheets/
     underage-drinking.htm.

6   Focus on The Family. "Why Kids Use Drugs." Accessed
     May 19, 2014. http://www.focusonthefamily.com/parenting/
     parenting_challenges/kids-and-substance-abuse/why-kids-use-drugs.
     aspx.

7   L. D. Johnston, P. M. O'Malley, J. G. Bachman, and J. E.
     Schulenberg, "Monitoring the Future National Results on Drug
     Use: 2012 Overview, Key Findings on Adolescent Drug Use,"

accessed May 19, 2014. http://www.monitoringthefuture.org/pubs/
monographs/mtf-overview2012.pdf.

8   Ibid.

9   National Institute on Drug Abuse. "Drug Facts: Inhalants."
     Accessed May 19, 2014. http://teens.drugabuse.gov/drug-facts/
     inhalants.

10   Harvard School of Public Health. "The Nutrition Source—Sugary
     Drinks." Accessed May 19, 2014. http://www.hsph.harvard.edu/
     nutritionsource/healthy-drinks/sugary-drinks/.

11   Nemours Foundation—Center for Children's Health Media.
     "Keeping Portions under Control." Accessed May 19, 2014. http://
     kidshealth.org/parent/nutrition_center/healthy_eating/portions.
     html#.

12   Centers for Disease Control. "Overweight and Obesity—A Growing
     Problem." Accessed May 19, 2014. http://www.cdc.gov/obesity/
     childhood/problem.html.

13   US Department of Health and Human Services. "2008 Physical
     Activity Guidelines for Americans." Accessed May 19, 2014. http://
     www.health.gov/paguidelines/pdf/paguide.pdf.

14   Henry J. Kaiser Foundation. "Generation M2: Media in
     the Lives of 8–18 Year Olds, 2010." Accessed May 19, 2014.
     http://kaiserfamilyfoundation.files.wordpress.com/2010/01/
     mh012010presentl.pdf.

15   American Academy of Pediatrics. "Media and Children." Accessed
     May 19, 2014. http://www.aap.org/en-us/advocacy-and-policy/aap-
     health-initiatives/Pages/Media-and-Children.aspx.

16   National Conference of State Legislatures. "Teen Pregnancy Prevention." Accessed May 19, 2014. http://www.ncsl.org/research/health/teen-pregnancy-prevention.aspx.

17   The Barna Group. "Teen Role Models—Who They Are, Why They Matter." Accessed May 19, 2014. https://www.barna.org/teens-next-gen-articles/467-teen-role-models.

18   Ibid.

19   Ibid.